Look at Us

Let's See

Here We Are

Look Hard, Speak Soft

I See, You See, We All See

Stop, Look, Listen

Beholder's Eye

Don't Look Now, But Isn't That You? (Us? U.S.?)

words by
WILLIAM SAROYAN

photographs by
ARTHUR ROTHSTEIN

A COWLES BOOK

The Eye Looks Out

It all starts with Narcissus seeing in a pool of water a face that turns out to be his own.

The eye looks out. All visibles are out, not in. But the eye is out, too, in all members of the animal family.

After the discovery of the optic reflection came the invention of the looking-glass, permitting the beholder to behold himself, which is the beginning of everything.

It is impossible to imagine man without eyes. He could never have become man had he not had eyes. It was having eyes and being able to see that gave him his form, style, and meaning, out of which he discovered, charted, and tried to understand the earth, nature, and the universe. Eyes in living creatures, but especially in man, compelled the human world, with all of its appurtenances—tools, weapons, dwellings; and all of its systems—religious, philosophical, scientific, economic, educational; and all of its arts—singing, dancing, story-telling, painting, sculpture, poetry, and so on.

Life is seeing. The sun did it, of course. The sun's heat and light for billions of years warmed matter into the condition of opening itself unto the sun. The eye is sun-made. Had there been no sun the story of the earth would be something else again entirely—but there *was* the sun, there *is* the sun. And there are said to be millions of suns farther out, most of them much larger than our sun.

Our sun. We have always loved it to the point of having it central to all faith excepting the latest and more sophisticated forms of it, such as that of Moses, Jesus, and Mohammed, to name only three of the six or seven hundred men who found it necessary to go into the matter of faith in a professional way.

In English Christianity sun and son have the same *sound,* at any rate. On that account alone Christianity will probably die last among the English-speaking peoples of the world. But whether forms of faith die or live, forever or for three or four centuries, the sun is always there to keep the eye open, and as long as the eye is open the chances are good for the mind to be open, and for the spirit to go forth in search of something more to see.

What the eye sees it sees instantly, but even while it is looking the thing seen is changing and the eye that is looking is changing and the sun is moving and the light of the sun is changing.

Poets used to howl with grief upon beholding a beautiful girl, for instance, because they knew her beauty would flourish only a short time, and then be gone forever. And nobody would be able to remember it. And it was too precious to be forgotten. So the poets put the beauty into words, into the mystic-scientific language of poetry. And so it was with song-makers and singers, painters and sculptors, philosophers and saints, dramatists and novelists, dancers and composers, each working in his own medium. People, mainly royal, were painted and drawn by hired portrait-makers. The thing achieved by means of drawing and painting was art, a special thing, frequently revealing even the ineffable in a man, woman, or child. But how many people could afford to hire a painter?

The camera was a long time coming, but even after it had arrived it didn't really step out and do its work in anything like the full and varied manner indicated.

Moving pictures are only just beginning to discover what they can do, after about seventy-five years. Science, research, libraries, archives, history, automation—I use the words freely—are all exploiting the camera in new and exciting ways: not to mention rocketry, and space exploration.

It is all to the end that what we see instantly can be seen again at our convenience precisely as it was seen in the instant, in the first place; to the end that we can begin to guess a little more accurately and meaningfully as to who we are, where we are, what we are doing, how we are changing, what we have made, what we have destroyed, and so on and so forth endlessly.

It is in our nature to look and to see. We thrive in this luxury—this never-ending feast. The more we look and the more we see, the more we want to look, and the more there is to see, and the more fine points there are to discover in everything it is possible for us to see. A daisy is a pretty simple flower until you begin to really look at it. A good photograph of a daisy will impel you to start looking at a real daisy more pointedly, and from that looking to look at all things more pointedly. The most difficult thing of all to see is an eye looking at (or into) your eye—because the eye is also a person.

Arthur Rothstein is a professional photographer. His work is straight, not arty. At their best, however, his pictures are works of art. Understanding the mechanics of the camera is likelier to make art than trying to understand the truth about God. The value of camera-pictures lies in their aesthetic neutrality. Before it is anything else a photograph is a fact. Then, comes its subject. And finally its identification—the picture is a work of art, a work of history, or both. It isn't necessary for a photograph to be both, but many of Rothstein's photographs are.

Putting words to pictures may seem a funny business, but that is precisely what man has done from the beginning—that is how he made everything he did in fact make, and how he came to find, measure, and try to understand everything else. New pictures impel new words, new variations of words. One picture is worth a thousand words. Yes, but only if you look at the picture and say or think the thousand words.

I like to look at pictures. I enjoyed trying to find the right words for each of these 101 pictures.

WILLIAM SAROYAN   74 RUE TAITBOUT PARIS   OCTOBER 12 1967   COLUMBUS DAY

Look at Us

Let's See

Here We Are

Look Hard, Speak Soft

I See, You See, We All See

Stop, Look, Listen

Beholder's Eye

Don't Look Now, But Isn't That You? (Us? U.S.?)

Hi, Doctor Varner.
Hi, Merle.
Hot enough for you?
Oh, I'll live through it.

Here's a man on the sidewalk of a small town greeting a younger man in overalls, that's all.

It happened twenty-five or thirty years ago, around noon.

A man's shadow is at his feet, almost.

Kansas.

The town called Goodland because the land *is* good—cereal land: wheat, corn, oats, rye, maize.

But this is one of the great American pictures of all time.

Farm people are delightful people, although not stylish, sophisticated, educated, or refined, to use their own words.

Their clothes are haphazard, and they themselves inside the clothes are lumpy and lopsided.

Their worldliness has a sensible if narrow range, from the house and farm to town and bank, merchant, county fair, church, picnic, and back.

Their learning is in practicalities related to land, weather, plants, and animals.

Their relationship to the creative world of change, ideas, and the arts is not intimate.

They're too busy with hard work to be sensitive to the revolution of the spirit.

This Iowa farmer and his wife look like the good things they have grown and hold.

The man is as simple as potatoes and as straight as corn, the woman is as round and full as a watermelon and red tomatoes.

And in each of them there is something of the size and steadfastness of the great tree before which they stand.

But the little farmer is not long for this world of reluctant labor and impossible taxes.

His little place will soon be bought out for a good price by the syndicate which will put thousands of acres under scientific cultivation, and the good farmer and his good wife will try living in a little rented house somewhere or in an apartment, putting a little garden in the backyard, or a few plants in pots, to remind them of their proper connection with the earth.

4

Here's Washington crossing the Delaware almost two hundred years after he actually did—three small American boys in a boat on the Delaware, each of them Washington himself: the small boy up front drumming for dear life, truth, and native land; the larger boy just back of him holding Old Glory; and the third boy pushing the boat along with an oar through the shallow water.

Well, what does it mean?

It means somebody is determined not to let everything slip away and be forgot.

Somebody is trying to get a tradition fixed.

The three boys are at a grand summertime moment, perhaps the 4th of July, and while they aren't experts at history and don't know too much about what happened, they *do* know Washington crossed the Delaware, fought the Red Coats of England, won the fight, and thereby became the founder and father of his country.

The hats made out of folded newspapers are good to see somewhere in the world again.

All kinds of things, certainly all kinds of hats, can be made out of newspapers by means of folding, but one hardly ever sees such foldings any more.

Pressmen of the Fresno Evening Herald fifty years ago wore a square hat made of folded newspapers, and these hats seemed more real and right than any other kind of headgear they might have worn.

The point is there are things to be done with old newspapers.

Orson Bean rolls one up, makes a few tears, and telescopes a fine tree straight up from the roll—very good to see, not a trick, just an illustration of the art of using old newspapers in a clever way.

History, and the news, yes, by all means, but after a man crosses the Delaware, he ought to have a hat to remove.

He was a rich man who affected love of the poor.

He enjoyed teasing the rich, who soon after he was elected began to hate him and to believe he was wrecking the nation and spoiling its masses.

From Russia, from Communism, he chose the ideas he believed were good and put them to work, and the ideas *did* work.

Labor benefited.

The needy, the aged, the ill, and the unemployed benefited.

And strangely even the rich benefited—they got richer.

He had a way of talking that appealed to ordinary people because it was in fact elegant, or high-toned.

He seemed to come from a kind of American royalty.

Before television, his fireside chats over the radio took him into every home and made of him a kind of Father figure, a role he encouraged and enjoyed.

Drafted soldiers imitated his radio talk about how he knew war, how he hated war, and how he would never, never send American boys into a foreign war.

At Tehran and at Yalta, Stalin used him shamelessly, exploiting his need to be loved, admired, respected; and as a result the War never ended.

Not that there is ever any such thing as Peace—there isn't.

But there are relativities in both of the grand abstractions—War and Peace, and the world had a right after the destruction of Hitler's psychotic-criminal Germany to enjoy a higher order of identification of man's real enemy, himself.

8   And a fuller awareness of what a struggle is for—intelligence.

If the name hadn't been put upon it, would anybody have known it was a bank?

And while the bricks were being laid to form its walls, would any farmer or his wife or his kids have known?

Might it not have been a grocery store, or more likely a general store, with everything in it that a small community of farming people might need—seed, feed, grain, flour, lard, frying pans, kettles, pots, and all the other things plain living needs?

But no, at the top of the little odd-shaped building the laying of the brick became decorative, to let everybody know that this was not an ordinary building, this was as special as a church, and in many ways not unlike it.

This was a bank, and so named over the entrance.

This was the home of mystery and magic, of the mightiest of the mighty, the home of money, which could work more miracles than any religion, saint, or messiah.

And it failed.

And the harvesting machine beyond the bank failed.

Only the weeds did not fail.

See the bank.

See the little red-brick bank.

See the little red-bank standing perfectly still in a great field with miles and miles of empty land all around it.

See the little red-brick bank all alone, no mother, no father, no brother, no sister, no President, no depositor, no robber, no money.

Say goodbye to the little-red-brick bank, goodbye and better luck next time—on the moon, maybe.

"The Union forever," the song says, "hurrah, boys, hurrah."

The Union was the nation itself in the time of the war between the states.

The Union is still the nation itself, although there is now also the Union of workers joined together to secure reasonable living adjustments in accordance with the continuously-changing economy of production, wages, security, and prospects for comfort and dignity in the future.

Management (the money) and labor (the producers) remain at war, but the nature of the war is improved, and an element of alliance has developed in both sides.

One needs the other, the nation needs both.

Here are four men who help produce steel.

Three appear to be from families that originated in central Europe, Poland perhaps, while the man with the moustache might be of Irish extraction, speculations which aren't entirely beside the point, although each is first of all an American and a worker.

Poles somehow fell to working in the steel mills, for instance, along with Hungarians, Czechs, and the Irish, the companies prospered, the whole nation benefited, but for a long time the companies did not volunteer to improve conditions and wages for the workers, and so they organized and demanded the improvements.

They are getting them.

There is no such thing as making conditions and wages too good for workers as long as the whole country is rich, and hundreds of thousands of its people are millionaires.

For longer than fifty years, half a century of rather insane, painful, magnificent, criminal, but now and then saintly time of the world, Isadore Baline, called Irving Berlin, wrote the words and music of American folk songs that scarcely anybody knew *were* folk songs, that everybody believed were Broadway or Tin Pan Alley songs, and three generations of Americans lived and died to their simple melodies and messages.

Boys and girls fell in love to his tunes, made love to them, got married to them, broke up to them, tried again to them, carried torches to them, left home to them, cried to them, laughed to them.

During the First World War he summed up a little of the national agony in a bugle call song in which the youth of the country moaned and groaned, Oh, how I hate to get up in the morning.

Oh, how I love to remain in bed.

That war ended, the world changed, and then along came World War Two, out of the very city that he had long ago chosen as his name, and this time humor and laughter gave way to homesickness and melancholy, in I'm Dreaming of a White Christmas.

The troops (and the nation itself) sang the song and lived by it.

Many good men died by it, the war ended at last, and every Christmas the song continued to be the first song of the season.

The Getaway is one of the most profoundly satisfying of human experiences.

It is frequently a matter of life and death—if you make it, you live; if you don't, you don't.

Many didn't.

They were systematically killed by the millions, as if each of them was not a man, a woman, or a child.

Their killers were other human beings—politicians, scientists, doctors, military men, office workers, record-keepers, guards, citizens, everybody in a whole nation, and finally the human race itself.

There was no charge against them.

They were put to death because they were alive, in the way, a problem to a criminal program of politics and war.

Their destruction is forever on the conscience of the human race.

A few escaped, to tell of it.

These are some of them.

Their faces do not suggest that they have forgotten what happened to their brothers and sisters, fathers and mothers, sons and daughters.

It is good to live, to survive, to escape from a deathly place, to arrive in a place of decent reasonableness, as these refugees have arrived in New York, but it is impossible to rejoice in one's own good luck.

That is not enough.

Which one is yourself?

Or is it ever again possible to be truly yourself?

There are a lot of fascinating facts and figures about the Statue of Liberty in New York Harbor and they should be looked up in an encyclopedia every now and then, but the biggest fact about this enormous statue is that immigrants from Europe by the hundreds of thousands saw it when they reached America at last and stopped at Ellis Island for processing.

The Lady with the Torch was very big, very beautiful, and surely meant something very big and very beautiful, perhaps freedom, perhaps sanctuary, perhaps protection.

The kids, grandkids, great-grandkids and great-great-grandkids of the immigrants sooner or later heard about or saw with their own eyes the Great Lady, and then she meant something else, something new, something more.

There are far larger statues in other harbors and at the top of mountains in other parts of the world, but they are generally statues of Jesus.

This Lady isn't worshipped, she was never human, she is a work of art, an American trademark, created and manufactured not in America but in France.

There is a winding stairway in the uplifted arm which I climbed the day after I first reached New York, and there is a small area of wall on which is written in ink: W. S. August 31, 1928.

Making the pilgrimage to the Statue was to honor my father, who saw it in 1905, went west in 1908, and died in 1911.

Why aren't more great symbols put about all over the country?

Gutzon Borglum's mountain bas-relief of the heads of four Presidents is a kind of midwestern marvel, and art, of sorts, as well—but not enough.

Great art—in itself and in its size—can do more for a nation than any four Presidents, ever.

In his View of Toledo the painter Domenikos Theotokopoulos who was called El Greco, The Greek, because he was a Greek, because he had gone from Crete to Toledo, painted earth, sky and clouds in a way that made his whole picture as much a landscape of the human soul as of Toledo seen from a distance.

In looking at the picture one felt that one was also seeing something of one's own self.

El Greco's vision was also the beholder's, and the painting was a reminder that the beholder did have such vision, and the painting was instruction in the usage of such vision.

Art is looking.

It is also seeing.

Art is in honor of the ability to see, and in memory of all that is always there to see.

There is nothing that is not worthy of notice.

Anything noticed is thereby transformed or transfixed into being a part of the grand unity which is, was, and will be.

Notice fixes the swiftly moving into a place in infinity.

But most of all looking is its own instant reward: seeing something clearly is having it.

If there is any real wealth, this is probably its truest form.

Clouds come and go, mountains start and stop, each is new and old suddenly, as grass and trees come and go, and water flows.

Something everlasting is happening every instant.

If you look carefully you can see it happening, even though the youngest mountain is a million years old and still growing.

Nations are not systems, they are people who love their land, sky, grass, trees, rivers and mountains.

There comes a time when it just won't do, you've got to get up and go, you've got to try some other place, you've got to make the break, now, in 1936, you've got to leave dry South Dakota and go to wet Oregon, for instance.

Here's the great nameless movie actor himself in the colossal Weather Bureau Production called South Dakota Drought.

Here he is thirty years ago, and the movie is still being shown on late-night T.V., but his car has long since fallen to antique pieces strewn carelessly along the Oregon Trail.

My name is 52–2409, you've seen me on a dozen highways, walking down hundreds of streets, in thousands of villages, towns and cities, bearing other numbers and names.

I am the Loner, the Rebel, the Traveler, the Seeker.

What's up ahead?

Man, *I'm* up ahead, waiting to start my real life, God helping.

The travail of man is secret, known only to himself in the instant of its highest intensity, leaving upon his visage a deepened line of patience, wisdom, and fortitude.

The faces of uncomplicated men, of all who live upon the land, close to nature, close to the elements in man's own unstoppable compulsion to survive, to occupy a place, to found a home and a family, to work and to produce, against all odds—are stories.

Dust he was, dust he is, and dust he shall be again, as he knows, as he has read in the one book he took with him in search of his own place and his own people, his own wife and kids, one of them walking with him through a storm of the earth's own dust, walking perhaps a little ahead of him, the other, the younger one, toddling behind, chasing after the father, protecting his eyes and nostrils and mouth from the air itself, now suddenly laden with the fine substance of the earth, a desolation he will perhaps remember that he experienced early in his life, although he may wonder if it were not dreamed, as so much of his truth was.

Dreams are never photographed, and man's most wonderful and terrible realities are hardly ever, and then almost by accident.

Oklahoma! a cheerful folk opera was called, which ran on Broadway and all over the country for twenty years or more.

Well, there was, there is, another Oklahoma, most likely without an exclamation mark, and very definitely inhabited by people—some of them eager to go on the stage some day, too, all of them something more than they had been, for the dust of Oklahoma they breathed.

Dust or no dust, we're going on, and our first destination is the storehouse for a supply of food in case the dust keeps coming for a long time.

The barber shop in America is a place worthy of the best notice of anthropologists, sociologists, economists, educators, historians, philosophers, poets, and dramatists.

First of all, it *is* a place, whereas in many countries barbers still ply their trade in the streets, under trees, or wherever there may be a customer.

Barbers talk, and their customers listen, as in the celebrated story Haircut, by the great Ring Lardner.

A good small-town barber can talk about anything, a good big-city barber cultivates keeping his mouth shut on all subjects: if anybody is going to talk, it has got to be the man in the chair, who is sometimes the President himself of the country, or the bank, or something or other.

One barber shop custom that is difficult to understand is the holding of the mirror to the back of the head, so that the man in the chair can see his haircut and nod his approval, even though my own honest reaction has always been, "Worst haircut I ever got, thanks a lot, I might have lost an ear."

Going to the barber shop, getting spruced up, is part of the American ritual of putting forward one's best face, for purposes of acceptance and success in the world, and to entitle a man to expect a second glance from a woman.

Poets earn their keep by teaching at schools and colleges.

Barbering might be a better idea.

Few barbers know how to give a haircut.

I have never known a barber to study the man and the head before starting.

A poet could clean up giving his customers real haircuts, with perhaps a recitation of his latest poem thrown in for good measure.

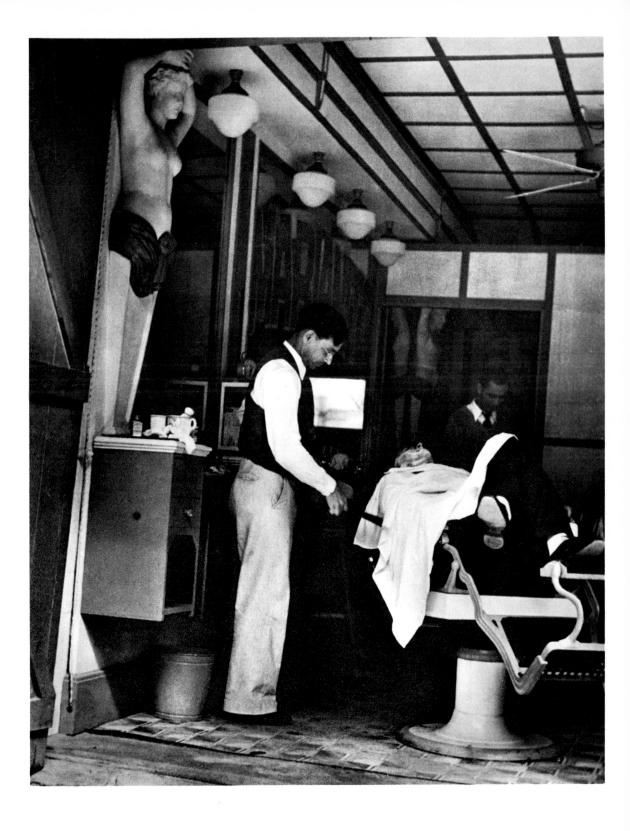

Shooting pool is one of the favorite activities of young men who have little or no aptitude or inclination for becoming President.

They tend to smoke, swear, gamble, and lie about where they have been.

Theoretically, the pool hall has always been the place where young men all over the country have started going wrong.

A place of idleness, inactivity, indifference, relaxation, peace, and happiness.

The table is the world, and the breaking of the racked balls is the establishing of an abstract problem, whereupon the players go to work solving the problem.

But the pool hall has been taken from the side streets and moved into the youth centers, with interesting wall decorations: an Indian design, and a basketball player.

The four boys here aren't typical—nobody ever is—but they look just right for the setting and the action.

The younger boys only want to move along to independence and freedom.

The older boys only want to finish the game in peace, so they can start a new game.

This is a picture of a pitcher or a pitcher of a picture, as one might say.

He is pitching for the New York Yankees, once invincible, now feeble, but always likely to come back, as every team of each league is likely to do, which of course makes both the game and the race for the league pennant and the World Series so exciting— stuff nobody but an American is likely to understand, but also stuff many Americans either don't understand or find boring and therefore can't be bothered about.

The fact is that baseball is one of the purest, most infinitely dramatic and complex of all athletic games.

A great game is the equivalent of a great work of art.

And the most important of the nine players is the pitcher.

At his best a pitcher is a demonstration of genius in action.

The complexities of a perfectly pitched game have not yet been fully explored, identified, or fixed.

Professional baseball has sharpened batting skills so effectively that disaster is not unlikely every time a pitcher gets the ball over the plate.

And yet some of the greatest batters just can't hit some of the greatest pitchers.

The trick of both batting and pitching is to be perfectly relaxed while being involved in effort that simply has got to be violent to be effective.

The mind and spirit have got to be relaxed while every muscle of the body is as tight as steel.

30   The great players manage it, making a contradiction uncontradictory, and reasonable.

Who is an infant?

Even after carefully considering the infant's mother, father, brothers and sisters, who is the infant?

Well, at the outset at least a few interesting facts are possible: sex, weight, and health.

After that, however, it is all unknown, although geneticists can make a number of guesses.

For the most part, however, the guesses are meaningless and useless: because it's too late now.

Here's a little girl in the classic position, so to put it, enjoying the admiration of a big sister and a big brother, both actually also little children, still unknown entities to their parents and certainly to themselves, although a good deal less unknown than the infant.

Who is she?

Who might she become?

How long will she live?

Where will she go and what will she do?

Who will she love, who will she marry, how many kids will she bear?

Will she dance in ballet, sing in opera, win the shot-put at the Olympics, act on the stage, be elected to the Senate, teach English at high school, practice medicine, be injured in an automobile accident, go mad, commit suicide, or die of old age?

Nothing is certain, so just thank God the kid seems O.K., and the world is still reasonably habitable.

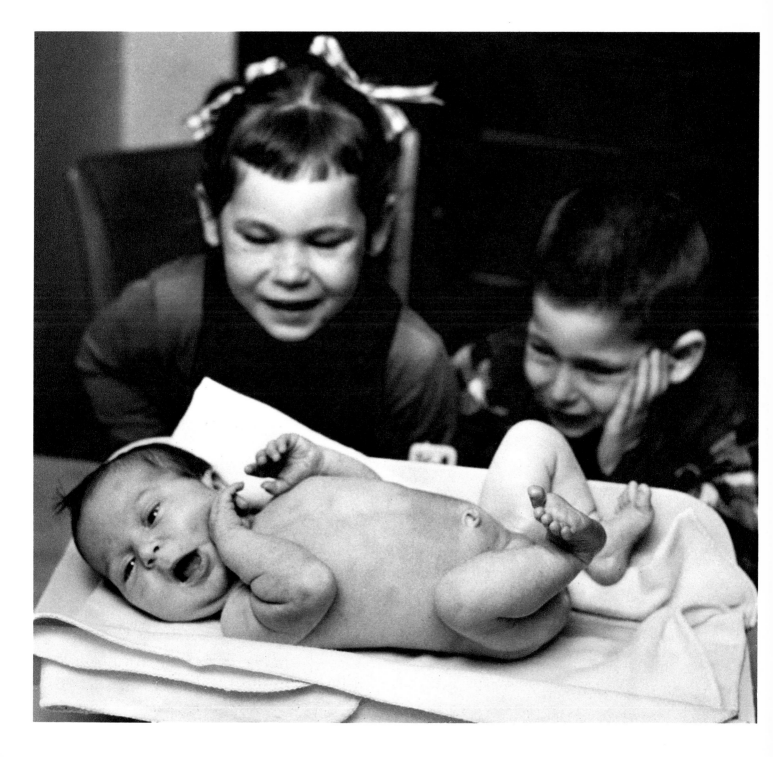

He is an old man with a long white moustache and beard coming down from what's left of the hair on his head, all of it the same texture and color.

He's a little lame now, needing crutches to stay on his feet and get around, in need of glasses, but still happy to put on work clothes in the morning.

Beyond him, almost invisible, are people, men and women, much younger than himself.

Well, who are *they?*

Members of the family, at a reunion.

He is being honored by a close-up photograph because he is the oldest surviving member of the tribe.

Eighty-eight?

So what?

I've still got a lot to learn.

West Virginia isn't the easiest kind of land to farm, and the seasonal patterns of the weather have been changing quite a bit during the past seventy years.

I think it's because the younger generation doesn't go to Sunday School.

A sudden thunderstorm with lightning is some kind of wrath, but try to tell that to these newcomers, and all they do is think you're superstitious.

Floods don't happen for nothing.

Somebody doesn't like the way we're bringing up our kids.

Thank God for the stars and stripes.

Everything that occupies space upon the earth is either a monument or a tombstone to something, if only to itself.

A tree stands as its own brave, proud, pitiful, or magnificent truth.

Its meaning is itself, for no tree is precisely like any other tree, even in a forest of trees of the same seed and breed.

Everything is like everything else, but each thing is its own incredible self.

Highly magnified grains of sand are seen to be real each in its own way.

All things are vulnerable to one thing, change.

Trees are sensibly turned into timber, or senselessly into debris by fire, storm, or flood, but nothing stops the tree at the source of its truth, in its immortal seed—neither fire, storm, flood, squirrel, bird, insect, accident, practicality, nor profiteering.

Always seed enough survives, to start again, beside the charred, broken, bleak tombstone.

Poets and painters have always celebrated trees, as well as all other things which hang on, including people.

Several of the slighter religions have formulated their dogma upon the reality of trees.

How like a tree is a man?

Apparently, not at all, except that each shares ultimate and inevitable forfeiture of itself to a whole, a tree to the forest, a man to the race.

Plants persist.

Even a cabbage is forever—in its truth and beauty—until it becomes sauerkraut, or an object of protest flung at a phoney.

These workers, bearing names like Thompson, Crawford, Murphy, Smith, are Anglo-Saxon Americans of Alabama, who suffer themselves to be carried deeply down into the earth where they break coal free from great geologic slabs and send them up to keep the industrial fires burning and the great machines of production turning.

It's hard work, it's dangerous work, every man knows somebody who died on the job, crushed or hopelessly locked in by a preventable or an unpreventable cave-in.

The wages aren't much, certainly not enough, all things considered, but these workers don't suddenly quit, pack up, and go to California.

You put in eight hours, you come up, another day has come and gone and you're free until early tomorrow morning.

One day at a time, and then you line up again, to be carried down to the job, or to pick up your wages which always come just in the nick of time to pay the bills and keep the house and family together.

That's what it comes to.

Somebody's got to do it.

Somebody's got to bring home the needed money every week.

The lining up is learned from the ants, it isn't a natural human compulsion or necessity for the achievement of order and procedure, but every man in the line of hundreds of men is an individual, living a life only he knows, for reasons only he cherishes, mainly the kids.

Hell, it's not too bad, there's all that comradeship, and some of the boys are real comics.

The jokes never stop.

The telling of old and new jokes goes on all the time.

The whole thing is a joke, isn't it, when you get right down to it?

Why shouldn't we smile?

38

We know what we know, don't we?

School days, who would ever guess that such days would come to be considered happy? Nobody worries as the schoolboy does.

Nobody is so at home in a classroom as a schoolgirl.

This is only slightly puzzling: girls and women tend to seek simple forms of social order, boys and men seem to need the fullest possible forms of individual freedom.

When a man is small and not permitted to vote for the way of life he wants, school is imposed upon him by his family, by society, and by the law of the land itself.

To fight them all is impossible, so he goes to school.

Huckleberry Finn is the first of the classic American school-hating boys.

There is a little of Huck in every American boy at school, up to about the third grade, after which a livable armistice is made, and a boy either tolerates what he dislikes, or discovers loopholes by means of which he is able not to permit school to interfere with his education.

These are fourteen boys and two girls at a public school in New York, and their teacher, a brave but surely misunderstood lady, possibly hated by some of the boys.

A growing man has got to have somebody to exercise his hate on, thank God a teacher is there for that purpose.

Who are these boys going to turn out to be?

A banker, a dentist, a lawyer, an accountant, a poet, a scientist, an astronaut, an actor, a mechanic, a clerk, a President?

How long?

How much longer?

When will it be our turn?

You guys had your chance and goofed, wait until we take over, you'll see the way the world *ought* to be run.

And then suddenly each of them is an adult and can't remember what he was going to do to make things right.

Or he's sure it can't be done, so forget it.

When the little ex-haberdasher of Missouri became President, a lot of people in America and all over the world groaned with anxiety, for he just didn't seem to be made of the stuff that that high office required, and the world was in the kind of mess that everybody knew wasn't going to be easy to get out of.

But soon enough he gave the impression that he could at least carry out the intentions of his predecessor.

He gave the order to drop two atom bombs on two real, live, Japanese cities, occupied by hundreds of thousands of men, women, and children.

No other weapon in the history of the world had destroyed so many innocent people in such a short time.

You *had* to be President to do a thing like that.

The Republicans ran a man named Thomas Dewey against him, the Public Opinion Polls and the newspapers predicted that Truman didn't stand a chance.

A Chicago paper even ran a headline: DEWEY WINS.

But Dewey didn't.

Harry did.

There is a National Game of naming Great Presidents, Near Great, Good, Average, Bad, Lousy, Criminal.

The fact is that the world itself, the human race itself, history itself, the nature of each of the nations of the world, no longer permits any man in public office anywhere even to give the illusion of being great.

It is quite simply impossible.

Since the turn of the century every President of the United States has been a little of each of the classifications in the National Game.

The office is now totally impossible.

It is virtually obsolete.

In the next twenty years severe but unavoidable changes in the executive government will be established—and about time, too.

These are men drafted into the Army of the United States, as I believe it is sometimes called.

They are being taught to salute in the manner preferred by the Army—by its high-ranking officers.

If they fail to salute in precisely the proper manner they are punished.

The punishment might be a big job of dirty work in the kitchen, the denial of an evening's pass, or shipment to the front, as it used to be called.

All the same, the mark of eminence among high-ranking officers in the Army is to salute in an extremely offhand manner, breaking all of the rules which have cost many a country boy or slum boy virtually his life.

The higher a man gets in the Army, if in fact he doesn't happen to start at the top, the more he affects being unbound by the Army's rules and regulations, the more he fools with the prescribed costume, throwing out stuff he doesn't like, and putting on stuff he does.

Having chosen regimentation as the arena in which to flourish such men proceed to affect independence, individuality, and even eccentricity.

A Mr. Patton, for instance, who was in fact officially a General, carried on like a cowboy in an inferior picture, swaggered about talking man-to-man to terrified kids who knew they weren't anywhere near to man-to-man baloney anywhere in the world except at home, now far away, and slapped down a shocked Brooklyn boy for having the nerve to behave for all the world like a yellow-bellied unAmerican coward.

Brave to the end, rebuked by the stupid press and the stupid public, transferred to another front, he was involved in a jeep accident, long after the end of the war, and was thereby prevented from dying in bed, where a Mr. MacArthur died, aged 99 or thereabouts, and a Mr. A and a Mr. Z will also eventually die great national heroes, every one of them.

Not a face in the crowd.

A cross for the Christian, a star for the Jew, no mark at all for the man who believed only in God—that is, in himself.

One is supposed to be deeply moved by military cemeteries, especially when they are in foreign countries, such as France, far from home, but the sorrowful fact is that the picture is so unavoidably one of uniformity and waste that one is actually only depressed by it.

The long rows of sticks over men who were killed by their unknown brothers, many of them also dead, seem to say, "Plenty more where they came from."

These are the known soldiers.

46　　　They might just as well be unknown, for all the difference it makes.

This little girl is six years old and eligible to try to blow out six small flames in one breath and make a wish, while her mother and her friends watch and wonder if she'll get her wish.

Everybody else will also make a wish, even though it isn't everybody's birthday.

Wishing is the great pastime of the young.

It isn't entirely unpopular with the old, either.

As for the birthday party, as such, many people are addicted to it, and not a few when they come to the age of fifty or sixty arrange for a big one in their own honor, with solicited tributes from relatives, friends, contemporaries, and important strangers.

Presidents throw big birthday parties for themselves, and all the wonderful people who live by invitations knock themselves out pulling strings to get invited.

It's a nice custom for kids, though, and entirely in order because they can't wait for enough years to go by to permit them to step out of the tyranny imposed upon them by the adult world, and to be free at last.

A mother is just fine, and a father is just fine, but who wants them forever, cluttering up the place with instructions, advice, reminders, laws, and orders?

It's a nice day because you give little presents and you get little ones, and there is
48 always ice cream and cake, funny hats, games, notions, and dressing up.

When sloppy and overbearing personalities on television ask little kids what they want to be when they grow up almost none replies that he wants to be a painter, or as the popular language puts it an artist; and yet nobody can say the nation hasn't given the art of drawing and painting a good try, for there is scarcely a community of five thousand souls or more in which there are not classes in art.

The more advanced students attend a live class, with a live model, perhaps because that is the traditional procedure for students of drawing and painting.

The reason so much teaching produces so little art is that the teaching is exterior instead of interior.

You get painting when you get a painter, and you get a painter from the inside of himself.

Even if he isn't especially good in the exterior things, the mechanics of painting, that is, a real painter's paintings will be paintings, not copies of the work of other painters.

Studying painting is a fine thing, however, even when the student is at heart a plumber or a bookkeeper: it will definitely improve his plumbing and his bookkeeping.

And it will certainly improve his eye for looking at good paintings, as well as for looking at people and things in general.

It takes a lot of character for anybody to have a room like John Marin's.

The room itself is a work of art.

Its very untidiness is art, the consequence of his own tireless creativity.

Seemingly at peace in the old wicker chair, enjoying a cigarette, apparently alone but actually in the midst of multitudes (of himself, at the very least), studying his latest finished work, he is actually busier than a board-boy on Wall Street, except that old John Marin is not chasing money, he's coming down the stretch in a very close race with Aesthetic Possibility.

Did he win, or did he lose?

You can be sure he lost, it is impossible not to lose, but look at what losing has brought to his face.

J. P. Morgan's winning in the Money Sweepstakes brought a midget girl to his lap near the end of his life.

But John Marin here sits forever in one of the wealthiest rooms any man has ever occupied, and is himself forever richer than all of the Big Money Boys put together.

And he wasn't by any means the greatest American painter of his day, either, but he *was* great, and that's enough.

What a strange thing a room is.

What a portrait of its occupant's soul.

The rich man's room is something in an antiseptic test-tube.

There is no dust in it.

Everything is in its place, as it is with a man in a coffin.

The cult of tidiness comforts the unborn dead, and permits the deranged to believe they have got everything in its proper place.

Poets, painters, sculptors, composers, and poor people with lots of kids live in houses full of rooms that are impossible to put right, because too much is going on in them, too much is growing, too much life is being lived in them.

What do you want?

That's the question.

You'll find the answer in the rooms of your house.

Here's a little of the Tennessee River, which like all rivers of the midwest eventually flows into the mighty Mississippi—two fine-sounding Indian words which long ago lost their strangeness, and seem to us perfectly American.

On the waters of the Tennessee is an old-fashioned excursion boat, of the kind Mark Twain piloted.

The foliage of the river banks has such summer charm that one is impelled to believe that one must drop everything immediately and hurry to where the river boats start their excursions, buy a ticket, and get on board.

A paddle-boat can slip through shallow water, but it can also become beached, and so the pilot has got to know his river.

If one of them is still running, all I can say is, I'm going to be a passenger at last next summer.

Racing along a super-highway in a crazy little car going a hundred miles an hour is some kind of fun, most likely.

Flying across the Atlantic at 32,000 feet, eating a fine supper, watching a ridiculous movie, and arriving in Paris after only six hours is also fun.

But steaming down the Tennessee—man, that's being intelligent, that's being brilliant, that's really dreaming.

This man has the tired tricky half-smiling face of all old poker players.

His purpose is to deceive the other players, and take the money.

No matter what the value of the cards he holds, his purpose is to deceive and to win.

If he has a good hand he wants the other players to think he is bluffing and really hasn't anything at all.

If he has nothing at all he wants the other players to think he is pretending that he has nothing at all but actually has a full house or something even better.

He does his deceiving with the same expression, the tricky half-smile which all gamblers (and a number of saints) eventually find on their faces.

But the other players (excepting suckers who play only for laughs) have the same expression, and each of them knows the way each of the others thinks and plays.

This is a small game, but small and big are interchangeable terms to gamblers: it's all one game, and if the truth is told it isn't really poker at all, it's life, it's character, it's survival, it's wit, intelligence, patience, insight, intuition, percentages, and last of all luck.

What's the good of good luck, for instance, if it isn't used, as when a player is dealt a full house or makes an inside straight and the other players throw their cards away and let him have his good luck?

For years in San Francisco I played poker with players like this old fellow.

I always had great luck and I always lost.

I didn't need the money as much as they did, and I didn't want to make poker a career.

But there are amateur poker players who work at it even more strenuously than the old-time professionals, and these players are frequently Hollywood actors, producers, and writers who long ago became millionaires.

They, too, need the money more than I do.

It's very interesting.

But then everything about money is interesting.

The rivalry between the Salvation Army and the Army of the United States has always been slight.

There is no West Point for the salvagers of souls.

Posthumous decorations are unknown, although successful daily work is probably rewarded with a high mark or a star after a name on a roster.

Vachel Lindsay wrote a jazz poem early in the century about General Booth, and Bernard Shaw wrote a funny play called Major Barbara (of the Salvation Army).

Others have written short stories about people who have served in the Salvation Army, or essays about the work of the Army, or biographies of some of its high ranking officers.

Still, the popular attitude toward the Salvation Army is patronizing—the Salvation Army is a joke.

But soon enough scoffers discover that the people who join the Army are not necessarily sick, deluded, demented, or weak.

The street-corner services of the Army provided a kind of world music nobody seems to have adequately appreciated.

The essential quality of this music was earnestness, but the music somehow always seemed delightful, a statement of humble hope for everybody, especially those who believed (or knew) they were hopeless.

The members of the band were so commonplace and undistinguished as to be eccentric.

The songs were the great songs of the Protestants.

A good American composer ought to do a whole Salvation Army symphony, as Brahms and Enesco, Bartok and Dvorak did symphonies of gypsies, peasants, emigrants, immigrants, and workers.

(The reason there is no real rivalry is that the armies are outmatched—the Salvation Army is in a class by itself, and long ago routed the Army of the United States.)

Georgia, Georgia, the song goes.

Well, *this* is Georgia and these are convicts on a chain gang.

If you've ever marched through Georgia, or ridden through in an automobile or a train, you may remember that most of the soil is red, and that here and there are great orchards of little peach trees.

But you probably never saw a chain gang in action, for the reason that they are put to work in remote places.

You saw chain gangs acted by movie stars in Hollywood, though, and it was always interesting.

It wasn't the real thing, this is the real thing.

A man is put into a Georgia chain gang not because he stole a little something or other from a store somewhere, or got into a fight, or got drunk and disorderly, but because he has no money, can't buy the services of a lawyer, doesn't know his rights, and figures he isn't much better off out of a chain gang, anyway, so the hell with it.

The laws, the enforcing of them, the courts, the lawyers, the judges, the jails and penitentiaries, the whole business of law-breaking and the taking of corrrective measures, or crime and punishment, is one great big fat rotten dirty diseased cowardly stupid criminal joke that just isn't funny.

The actor playing the part of the Governor of California, with his hard and pinched nose and mouth, campaigned openly in favor of capital punishment.

Oh, it's a great big state, and if he can save a couple of billion dollars by cutting allotments to the schools, and sending a lot of dirty murderers to the gas chamber, he will surely have left this world a nicer place than what it was when he found it, won't he?

(And just wait until he's President, Heaven forbid.)

The Boardwalk at Atlantic City, but it could be at Coney Island, or anywhere else, because it's the spirit of the place that counts, and the spirit of it is caught in the airy candy made by a spinning machine that flings sugar at high speed in a circle until an ounce of it becomes a great fluff of stuff gathered around a paper cornucopia, which kids like to hold and eat as they walk.

The whole thing is scarcely one solid mouthful, but that's all right.

This brother and sister have broken away from the rest of the family and are happily on their own, each perhaps with a whole dollar to spend.

They're from somewhere else, nicely dressed for the holiday at the seashore, and it's great to be there.

Trapeze flyers belong to the family of dancers, except that the dancing they do requires split-second timing in order to avoid disaster.

People at circuses do not see but surely suspect the intense concentration going on in all of the flyers just before and during the execution of a very complex problem of geometry, physics, space, motion, and time.

The greater the flyers the more effortless the achievement of the near-impossible seems.

The Arabs, who started so many things, started trapeze flying, as they did bull fighting, two profoundly graceful dance rituals in which the defiance of death designs the choreography.

What impelled them to do it?

The desert and slow time, perhaps; an impatience about coming face to face with the greatest friend or enemy, death; but it is probably more likely that both of these incredibly imaginative rituals are essentially religious, to the glory of God—to astonish, delight, and compel His respect and admiration for puny insignificant man.

Let us consider in comparison our own Western imaginative achievements of dance: baseball, football, and basketball.

Each is magnificent, beautiful, and satisfying both to play and to witness, but in none is there anything like the proud and lonely confrontation of fragile man and ruthless death.

Isn't the soul itself the greatest trapeze flyer of them all, from self to infinity?

At the end of the mortal roundtrip the trapeze swings low, the traveler latches on, rides to the top, lets go, reaches out, and this time at last there is no return.

There goes nobody, there goes anybody, there goes—is it possible?—me.

He was one of the generals elected to the Presidency, but he was no Jackson, no Grant, and certainly no Washington.

He had difficulty putting anything, however simple, into spoken words.

He frequently sounded like Professor Irwin Corey, and it was just this quality of indecision, of postponement of reaching a conclusion about anything, that had served him so well as the Supreme Commander of the Allied Forces in World War II.

It was a good idea to talk about things and not do them as long as possible.

When things were at an impasse he stepped in and started talking.

Hours and days and years later, while he still talked, tempers cooled, memories failed, and something like harmony was restored—among his own generals, and among the generals and politicians of England and France.

I have heard people say that he was very nearly the worst President of all.

And their reason for this opinion is interesting: he did nothing, he simply did nothing.

This could be a good thing, as a matter of fact, but it may be that it was his way of doing nothing that was unfortunate.

He had a heart attack while in office, and one instantly thought of his Vice President, a man named Nixon.

And then he had an intestinal condition that required surgery, and again one thought of Nixon, but the man had no luck at all.

Some Vice Presidents do and some don't, that's all.

Here is a summertime picture of a kind of heaven that deserves to be noticed, cherished, photographed but best of all, if possible, to be painted by somebody with the fire of life in his skull and skill, like Van Gogh.

An American heaven of golden wheat covering miles of gentle hills and meadows, at harvest time, in the wide wonderful state of Washington.

This harvesting combine is one of the oldest, long since out of date, but beautiful still to behold in action, sixteen horses, although at first glance there seem to be only eight: four abreast actually, and notice where the driver sits, away out in space, away from the racket of the combine, so he can holler instructions, encouragement, or admiration to the horses.

Wheat, more wheat, more and more wheat every year, because there are more and more people every year to eat it.

And still they come, and still there isn't enough wheat to go around.

Mother and Child.

He's a Sergeant in the Military Police, he's hearty, a good eater and drinker, he's got the beef to put down bad boys, he can be rough and tough when necessary, but he's still his mother's son, and she's proud of him.

Out of the Army what would he be?

A Deputy Sheriff?

A cop?

What happened, son?

What happened, mother?

War?

Is that what happened?

We're certainly doing our level best to make things turn out the way the people in the government say we've got to see that they turn out.

The American version of Santa Claus is a fraud that no kid in his right mind wants to expose, because the great myth is too useful to cast out any sooner than time is sure to cast it out in any case.

Santa Claus is performed every December by tens of thousands of virtually unemployable old gentlemen throughout the land, mainly in department stores, where kids line up to be received by him, as by a King.

The job of playing Santa Claus to a lot of little total strangers is a very hard job, for each kid has something to say that compels a reply, and quite a few of the kids ask questions that aren't easy to answer.

Magicians know that kids are not easy to deceive, and yet very few kids feel impelled to see through the obviously phoney white beard to the old gent who frequently smells of tobacco, whiskey, unemployment, and not of snow at the North Pole.

Kids prefer to join the conspiracy of pretense and deception, for they *do* suspect that it is for a good cause.

The poorest kid seems to know there are still poorer kids and that the pose and pretense of Santa Claus is not really for himself but for those other less fortunate kids.

And he really feels they should get some of the things they need from Santa Claus, from Christmas, from God, from adults, from charitable organizations, from the government, from somebody, from somewhere.

For half a century everybody has complained that Christmas is big business.
Of course it is, but so is sickness, pain, love, health, pleasure, and finally death.
There is no need to boycott Christmas and its clown Santa Claus on that account.
What price tag can be placed on the little girl's wonder and joy in being cuddled by Santa Claus, obviously phoney as he is, but at the same time unassailably, supremely, magically real.

A song of some of the black people of America said, "Nobody knows the trouble I've seen. Nobody but Jesus."

That is, nobody but the singer himself, nobody but the singer's own secret companion and comforter, or more accurately nobody but nobody, since nobody is able to see himself solely as himself, being able only to see others.

Only some of the black people sang the song, and sing it still, because its words and music are compelled not by color but by contrast.

It is a song of the hopeful who might otherwise be hopeless, for having so little, whether black people, white people, blended, or blending people.

A little girl in a glassless window of an unheatable, uncoolable shack set upon the red soil of Alabama is near having the interior wings of an angel not because the color of her skin is black but because all other means of transportation are beyond her range of experience.

She has got to use wings or she can't go.

She is also actually as much her white sister as she is herself, each not knowing the trouble of the other.

Behold the poor little black girl in the poor little Alabama house, but look carefully, and suddenly she is a young queen, not on a barge on the Nile a thousand years ago, but right where she is and right now.

She's wealthy beyond telling, having the head and hands of patience and pride, without which survival would have been impossible.

She's there, still, and whole, with memory itself defining the parts of her face: brow, eyes, nose, ears, lips, and chin.

What movie is she the leading lady in?

The one that happens ten million times a day in total secrecy, unproduced, undirected, unwritten, but more real than anybody's The Greatest Story Ever Told, The Bible, or Quo Vadis.

The colleges and universities are everywhere in every state and every city—land-grant colleges, state colleges, city colleges, private universities, religious universities, crackpot universities, experimental universities—all to the end that men may find out, may study, may learn, may become educated, as the saying is.

And it works, it isn't a fantasy, a falsehood, a foolishness, a flop, a failure—the idea works, it makes sense.

Everybody who goes to school comes away at least knowing a little more than he knew when he first went there.

But of course many who do not go to school appear to have known more from the beginning than many who went to school for thirty years or more, but that's another story.

The purpose of the universities and colleges is to prepare boys and girls for the world.

Graduation exercises are called commencement, to mark the moment when the students leave the hallowed ground of the school and race pellmell to the profane ground of the world, as these three graduates are doing.

They can't wait to get out there to the dirty world—to three martini-lunches with other professional men—dentists, lawyers, engineers, chemists, doctors, accountants, bankers, insurance agents, and so on and so forth.

To board meetings at which the animal snarls of ambition are cleverly concealed under cheerfully spoken but insincere compliments about rivals.

To sudden flying trips from Akron to New York, or from Birmingham to San Francisco, or from Minneapolis to Madrid, attending to the business of the world.

To membership in country clubs, which exclude Jews, Negroes, Mexicans, Arabs, Chinese, Eskimos, Communists, Mormons, Buddhists, Poets, and Workers.

Twenty years ago nobody here was born, even, but now here they are, students at a great university, and they want to know how long falsity is going to be sworn by, lived by, died by—and for what reason?

Is it to the end that a lot of ambitious third-rate men may have the illusion of importance and power for a short time?

Here's youth, demanding a decent world to live in, so they can believe in themselves, in love, in continuity, in the home, in the family, in working, in the possibility of a life without fear, harassment, interference, or criminal demands like, "You, come over here now, be a soldier now, train like a dog, sail to Asia, get out in the jungle."

If you are shattered by an explosion, so what?

It was for your country, and you know what your country is, don't you?

This is a protest against the government—the desperate, anxious, confused, bedeviled, over-worked, God-loving, church-going, criminal, pathetic, ambitious, powerful, rich, stupid, rotten, crooked government.

There are grown men and women of some intelligence who feel that the boys and girls at universities who protest are Communist, Chinese, sexually depraved, irreligious, unbathed lazy bums.

But the answer is that even if they were, what's that got to do with the protest?

Is anybody else doing anything about anything anywhere?

If the kids also can be bullied into not protesting, the jig is up, isn't it?

Everybody has seen beef brains at the butcher's.

These are human brains in the collection at Cornell University, being studied by a neurologist.

You can't quite know the personality or style of a man from a look at his brain, but the scientist can know if there was anything in his brain that made him live and work the way he did.

If you look at the neurologist's head and then at his gloved hand, you know there is a brain in each.

CORNELL BRAIN COLLECTION

Mother and Child again.

For centuries the theme has fascinated the greatest painters and sculptors of the world, both religious and secular: the theme of the continuance of the race against all odds, at all times, in all places.

The artist has always looked upon these two with love and reverence: the source and the issue.

This mother is helping her child to walk.

The child is happy, laughing and waving.

She has no idea that where she lives is not much.

To the child that place is as much as any place could ever possibly be—because the mother is there, and because the father is there, and the child can see the mother and the father too.

They live in the Blue Ridge Mountains of Virginia, most likely near the Trail of the Lonesome Pine.

Poor people?

Oh, they need a good forty or fifty thousand dollars, no doubt about that, but they're not poor.

They're there, they're still there, that's worth something not to be measured in terms of money at all.

Here we go now learning something new, something more, moving a little farther along the road that has no end—stuff and ways, conditions and meanings, problems and solutions, facts and fantasies, right and wrong, truth and untruth.

Well, this little boy whose very face is happy acceptance of the probable importance of learning, this fellow is going to make a pretty good showing, not just at school but everywhere else, for he was born with his good luck.

He has printed on glass a problem and its solution in the new math: 6 red cars equal —what *do* six red cars equal?

One suspects that one will never know, but the boy knows.

Six red cars equal six red cars—that's the starting point.

Then, six red cars equal a lot of other things, as you please, some in the language of the new math, most in the language of poetry, statistics, economy, finance, travel, highways, places, speed, safety, danger, accidents, injuries, deaths, employment and money, profits and losses—for six thousand red faces.

I'll get this straight if it takes me two minutes.

If God isn't watching, what is He doing?

This is His territory, isn't it?

There are places of culture not related to art in the traditional (and frequently stuffy) sense.

Kids go to these places with an unfailing instinct about where to put their admiration.

A blacksmith's shed with its living fire in the forge, its anvil, tongs, horseshoes, miscellaneous metal scraps, metal-cutter, vise, easy order and disorder, is such a place.

On the wall blackened by soot are horseshoes hanging from nails, bits, harness parts, saddle parts, and other pieces of metal so perfectly and sensibly shaped as to seem symbols in a mystic language of grace and utility.

And of course the blacksmith himself, with his powerful hands and arms, his knowledge of fire (accelerated as needed, and in ready repose), his expert timing in where and when and how to hammer molten metal to give it its desired shape.

Such a place is a banquet for a small boy's hungry eyes.

The seeming casualness of the blacksmith at work is a demonstration of unassuming anonymous superiority that is pleasant to notice, impossible to forget, and necessary to hope may one day be the style of the witness in whatever work he may find himself involved.

And of course there is the smell of the place: coke fire, soot, cinders, and seared and singed hoof-cartilege.

And there is the loud whisper and hiss of red-hot metal dipped into a tub of water, and the ring of hammer upon cooling metal.

If the witness is lucky he may even hear a few words of talk or song from the blacksmith himself as he does his work, or performs his art.

Near, unseen, is a horse to shoe, with a farmer or a gentleman rider standing by.

This is art in action, in its own gallery.

Soon a new sculptor will take the blacksmith's whole wall, give it a fancy name, and from it make his own name and a couple of thousand dollars, selling the wall to a Manhattan millionaire for his penthouse.

The memory of water is deep in man.

Kids love water as if it were a parent.

In beholding fish, whether in the rock pools of a stream, or half-hidden among the shallow reeds of a brook, the eyes of kids fill with wonder, as if they were beholding dear members of the family, or perhaps themselves in another form.

Getting to a body of water, getting to the banks of a stream or to a lake, or to the seashore, is not unlike reaching home—the old home, the abandoned home.

The feel of water upon the entire body is unique—nothing else is like it.

The embrace is total.

At the seashore, the great body of water has a rocking action that is central to all livingness—the law of opposites, in, out, back, forth, light, dark, soft, hard, alive, dead, and so on and so forth.

Kids near water whoop for joy, run, jump, dance, laugh, and sing, as if they might be sophisticated pagans defying all restraint upon the naked soul, which for a moment has the form of a small new body.

Almost every painter of genius has worked with the special light at ocean beaches, as this light penetrates the naked bodies of running kids, but there is one painting by George Bellows, an American, that burns with the strange love in living things for water and air —a livingness that is always very near but inaccessible, ineffable, and beyond being embraced.

O boy, Freckles in his fine jacket and white gloves, dancing with a great big girl, and Sparrow with his name-label pinned to his lapel standing as far off from La Belle Butte and still be dancing, what are they doing to the boys of the country, what are the mothers and aunts doing to Tom and Huck and all the others?

This is serious business.

Something's going on in the nation.

Mothers (and perhaps fathers, too) want boys and girls to be so nearly alike and comfortable about it that they can meet and dance as if it were nothing which it isn't, because boys are boys and girls are girls.

Just don't forget that there isn't a village in the nation that hasn't got a money-making school for social dancing—Arthur Murray, Buddy Ebsen, Fred Astaire, and others.

Millions of dollars in business every year.

For what?

Dawncing?

Dahncing?

Hell no, personality, freedom, fun, frolic.

Put a woman into a man's arms, the rest is up to him.

Anything can happen, although nobody discovered penicillin from having danced with a large lady at The Alhambra Ballroom Under the Stars on Highway 101 Just East of Venice on the Blue Pacific Where Time Meets the Tide From Avalon.

(Remember?)

The electric guitar did it, most likely, or at any rate helped: turned the new singers loose in the world, to sing the new songs, to make the new rhythms and sounds.

Elvis Presley in the mid-1950s got the ball rolling, winning from the traditional popular singers all people under sixteen, and most people over: but especially the screaming girls of eleven or twelve.

And then something a little unexpected happened: from Liverpool, a peculiarly unpromising English seaport city, came four rather funny-looking boys who called themselves a name out of Kafka: the Beatles.

They didn't resemble Beatles especially, although at first there was a suggestion of an unattractive insect in their appearance.

That appearance didn't change, but soon it seemed attractive in a strange unaccountable way.

They became a kind of Quartet-Messiah.

They were the saviors of inarticulate but desperate kids all over the world, but especially girls on the verge of sex.

And then it became an epidemic.

In ten or twenty years history will begin to understand what happened, but one thing is already clear: these are rebels, these music-makers are rejectors of the world they did not make, did not help to make, don't want, and refuse to have rammed down their throats.

They are past being bullied into conformity, or embarrassed into taking up arms against some fantasy danger or enemy.

They want to cool it—make songs, sing them, buy and wear clothes they prefer, let their hair grow, and invest their money: the Beatles, the Rolling Stones, the Mamas and the Papas, Sonny and Cher, the Grateful Dead, the Jefferson Airplane, and so on and so forth endlessly.

What's so bad about kids making music?

This clambake is notable for the kids in attendance and for their eagerness to get to the comestibles, so to put it, for the kids of the middle-class and the well-to-do are famous for their picayune, picky, tricky, troublesome, and anarchistic relations with food on the table.

They don't like to eat for some reason, possibly because there is always so much excellent food excellently prepared and served.

The children of the poor do not have to be urged to eat.

The children of the rich do not have to be told to take it easy on the meat.

But here at the clambake these kids seem to be eager to get to the lobsters and clams.

Is it because the lobster is such an astonishing assemblage of extraordinary parts beautifully balanced in one amazing living object?

Even rich kids don't eat lobster every day, certainly not out of doors at the beach.

Clams on the other hand have another order of aesthetic and culinary appeal.

A shut clam is something like a rock or egg, which when boiled opens up to a very nice taste of the sea.

The clambake is another American ritual in which the sea and a little of the life in it is loved and honored.

The one thing that starts at the beginning and stops at the end is eating.

No wonder cookbooks are perennial best-sellers, second only to The Bible, or, Insomuch as ye must eat in any case, for the love of God make it good.

He just barely—just barely—beat out Nixon, and the nation breathed a sigh of relief, because this boy was youth itself: superior, handsome, swift, brilliant, earnest, unafraid, determined, and bubbling over with a lot of good ideas.

The United States was young again, or perhaps it was young for the first time.

There was a sense of youth and confidence in the air.

His press conferences were spirited and amusing—he answered all questions with great skill, apparent honesty, and a lot of humor.

There was always a great roar of laughter at least once at every conference, generally at the expense of the little lady from Maine with the high-pitched voice and the sweet concern over irrelevancies, May Somebody.

He had a thousand days in office and then was unaccountably, unbelievably shot dead through the back of the head.

The people of the whole world were stunned.

A lot of people became hysterical.

Some actually got sick.

Many openly wept.

Many went to churches to kneel and pray.

Some wrote poems.

Some sent telegrams to his widow or to his parents or to his brothers or sisters.

Many wrote letters to newspapers.

But he was dead, before his time, his probable stature forever unknowable, and his achievement while in office awfully colored by a lot of emotionality.

An unfortunate and morbid fascination with his assassination, plotted, or willy-nilly, as the Government insists, is big business in the publishing world.

All of his closest associates have brought out books about him, in which he fares better than well.

History is beginning to glance at him in cool perspective.

None of the gossip about him, however, has so far been put into print, even as gossip.

The Manned Space Center in Houston, Texas.

The scene is meant to approximate (if such a thing is possible, and it isn't) a little of the landscape of the Moon.

The piece of machinery is a Lunar Exploratory Module.

The man is a World Man, or Astronaut.

He didn't arrive on the Moon *in* the Module.

The Module landed in a way I'll never know, and the Astronaut arrived in the same kind of way.

(Only so far it hasn't happened.)

The porous volcanic rock strewn about the legs of the Module are from our earth, but it is guessed that the surface of the moon is probably composed of such forms and such substances.

Probably not, would be more like it, though.

If it is possible to get to the moon, it is important to do so.

No matter what the cost is, no matter how the money spent might be used in other projects, it is important to get there—nowadays, as soon as possible.

Up to now travel to the Moon has been imaginary.

From now on it is going to be another story—unimaginative, purely scientific.

What are we doing it for?

What are we *really* doing it for?

The theory is that it is to extend the frontiers of knowledge.

And of course this is true.

But we are also doing it just in case there is a military (offensive or defensive) advantage in it.

The biggest most expensive national action always has this element in it.

All governments are cowards.

They are scared to death of all other governments.

Who will the first man on the moon be?

Each of us.

Away back in 1908 Mr. Arthur Brisbane wrote one of his characteristic editorials for his boss William Randolph Hearst entitled, Did We Once Live on the Moon?

We must have, or we wouldn't be such lunatics now.

What can I say?

What in the name of Blessed Jesus can I say?

O my wife, my daughter, my son, my father, my mother, my brothers, my sisters, O my friends, my enemies, my nation, my people, my world, O my life, I was the One, wasn't I, the new one, the young one, the wise one, the kind one, and there was so much for me to do for each of you, so much I wanted to do, so much I believed I could do, so much that somebody ought to have done long ago, so much that needed to be done before it was too late, and then it was, it was too late, what can I say, what can I say?

He never knew what hit him.

He didn't have time to be surprised and disbelieving, even.

Suddenly everything stopped, and there was running and amazement and pain and anger and sorrow, and then everything was the same as ever, everybody who was still there was still there and everybody had to move along the same as ever and nothing was different, nothing was changed.

Who did it?

Was it one man, or two, or three, or a conspiracy of three million, or thirty-three million, or fate, or only an unfortunate accident?

Or was it an Old Testament kind of sacrifice, secretly plotted in the counsel halls of mystery where purposes are unspoken and unspeakable, to tell the human race something it ought now at last to know, in a language beyond the realm of the known, a language plain but almost impossible to decipher, apparently meaningless, definitely unreasonable, forever astonishing.

Statues and monuments are a poor substitute for recognition, respect, understanding, and love for somebody no longer abroad in the streets and halls and council chambers, but they're better than nothing.

No village, town, city, or metropolis should be without them, for kids must know that every now and then there *is* such a thing as a man who is something more than other men.

In the earliest days of the business of putting up statues, the great men were on horses, but in our day one scarcely sees a great man at the wheel of an automobile or in the back where the great men tend to ride.

The horse, yes, the automobile, no—what is the meaning of that?

The most popular posture of a great man is sitting, as Lincoln sits here, in Washington.

Not far from Westminster in London he sits again, and so it is also in San Francisco.

You would think Lincoln did nothing else.

He is never shown walking in great strides, and one certainly suspects that he not only did a lot of walking, he *needed* to do more than most men, simply to keep from going to pieces.

The fact is that Giacometti's elongated works suggest the *quality* of Lincoln alive much more than any of the works in America, unmistakably Lincoln because of the melancholic brooding face and shaggy head.

Is there anybody like him anywhere in the nation now?

A lot of imitators, of course, especially among the brethren of the stage, but not in the government.

He had sons, and they weren't like him, and grandsons, and they aren't like him, so when will the world see another Lincoln?

Tomorrow maybe, maybe never.

It's probably just as well, because he might not make it at all this time.

They'd say he ought to see a psychiatrist.

Saturday night, what a night is Saturday night.

Freedom at last for a moment, part freedom, at any rate, enough to make the enslavement of the rest of the week at least tolerable.

What you do is shave, bathe, put on the best clothes you have, walk to town, stand on the corner, maybe something will happen, maybe something great will happen, but what would that be, what could that possibly be?

Would everybody in the world suddenly become black, so nobody would need to notice that somebody else is different?

Would everybody have a perfect right to feel as good as everybody else, about who he is and what he has in mind?

This is as good as I can make it.

Maybe it'll fetch me a good wife some day, and we'll have some boys and girls.

Now or never, this is my chance.

Tonight may be the turning point of my life.

A secret initiation into a secret organization, society, club, clan, fraternity, brotherhood, is suitable for boys and young men, one might say, were it not that one remembers that it was in boyhood and early manhood that the spirit was most vitally concerned about honor, truth, humanity, intelligence, democracy, freedom, individuality, sense, and the hope of a decent blending together of all of these desirable things in the man himself.

Thus, one is not permitted to feel or say that this sort of wearing of hoods and robes, this sort of candle-burning, arm-raising, oath-taking, mumbojumbo-speaking—is all right.

For ants, bees, sardines, bacteria, and germs, perhaps, but not for men.

If it were for fun, for laughs, as a criticism of adults, of the pomposities, absurdities, dishonesties, inequities of the great bodies of government, law, education, science, and so forth, this occasion would be one to applaud, respect, and enjoy.

But these poor lads, each of them potentially a fine useful member of the human race, of society in general, of his neighborhood, of his family, each potentially a father, are having no fun at all.

Each is confused by the imitated foolishness being earnestly perpetrated upon three younger outsiders with raised arms and brandnew haircuts—welcome to the fools' forum, boys.

Dancing girls are central to most if not to all of the tribes and cultures of the world, from the earliest times to the present, and very likely to the end of human time, for when the girls stop dancing, or their dancing does not impel the boys to turn away from hunting, whether for meat or money, human time will have come to the end of the line.

This is scarcely conceivable, however.

Girls walking down a street are dancing in the world itself, as every boy in every American town who has ever stood on a corner knows.

Girls standing behind a cash register in a coffee shop are dancing The Awfy Hop at the Coffee Shop, and it's part of a great national ballet.

This beautiful ballet dancer is Tanaquil Le Clerc who, like all ballet dancers, began training as a small child in order to be able at the age of nineteen or twenty to perform in Swan Lake, for instance.

Classical ballet belongs to another age and culture, but it has survived because the human race does not relinquish its memories without a struggle.

Why should it?

Those were the days, weren't they? They're gone forever but the memory of the dance lingers on, as the saying is.

Dancing has never been far from religion, but it has always been a little nearer to sin, or to the hopeful prospect of it, so that there is always a righteous anxiety on the part of ailing people to the latest dances and dancers.

They see sex in every little movement.

They are at least a little more right than they are wrong.

They just don't know how to dance.

The Dance of Life is the way Mr. Havelock Ellis put it.

All dancing comes from an awareness that life does in fact end.

Something's going on here in Williamsburg, Virginia, a colonial city restored by the Rockefellers.

Well, kids are going on, time is going on, light is going on, love of the past is going on, but most of all a happy and healthy involvement in the living present is going on, especially in the boy leap-frogging over the white colonial post, the boy with the T-shirt on which the word Rebels is printed, the boy with the camera, and the girl wearing the colonial hat, looking at the older girls riding in the two-horse carriage.

It's now in old Williamsburg, not yesterday.

A summer day of shadows.
Everybody and everything has a shadow.
Every boy and girl walks eagerly with his old pal, the summer shadow.

The coachman in his smart colonial costume waits for the procession of kids to pass, and the passengers faced away from the kids turn to look.

Something's going on, something more than just kids crossing a street, something possibly more than anybody can guess, and perhaps only the two fine horses do not feel it in their bones.

110　　　　American life is going on.

The building itself is like a loving child's prayer.
The church was built by and for Mexicans and Indians, in New Mexico.

It belongs to another time, but it is definitely in the right place, where space is great, the sun is hot, light is sharp, and shadows fall clean and clear.
The worshipping inside the church is simple, total, peaceful, and not unlike the worship of early cattle in early barns at eventide.

It was Calles who tried to drive the Mexicans away from the church, to liberate them (he thought) from their terrible imprisonment in the church, their resignation to their paltry lot in the world because of their comfort and wealth in the church and its promise of heaven.
He failed, totally.
And it was correct that he did.
Just supplement the church with worldly things until the people can decide for
themselves where their truth and comfort lies.

The American ritual of going to church originated in New England.

The ritual made sense on all accounts, spiritual and temporal.

Everybody bathed, put on the Sunday clothes, and walked to church, the inside of which had an atmosphere of space and peace decorated by light through colored glass.

The church was also a theatre presenting a play in which the basic form was well-known: organ music, opening hymn by the choir, prayer, hymn, responsive reading, announcements, collection, sermon, the singing of another hymn by choir and congregation together, and benediction.

The sermon was the unknown element in the play.

For a kid to stay after Sunday School for the sermon, there would have to be a pretty good reason: orders to do so from his parents, or by his own choice because he enjoyed the minister's way of talking.

Many ministers long ago fell to talking in a kind of whine which they apparently believed was Christian, but was actually a kind of Actors Studio performance of the role of Minister, a cover-up for empty words and ideas, irritating, monotonous, sleep-inducing.

Nowadays, though, ministers are known to be men, and they are expected to speak that way.

What do you tell a minister when you shake his hand after the sermon?

Great?

Lousy?

Thanks?

Keep trying?

Take it easy?

Or what?

Well, a sensible man leaving a church, shaking the hand of a minister, doesn't

really need to say anything.

Is that a framed photograph of Clara Bow just back of the Postmaster of Old Rag, Virginia, or is it a photograph of his daughter, or his son's wife, or a picture of a pretty girl, unknown?

It doesn't matter, the Coliseum of Rome is also there on the wall, another order of round and imperishable beauty.

And then to make it all serene, there is the religious card with picture and text, at a cost perhaps of twenty-five cents: Christ is the Head of this House, the Unseen Guest at Every Meal, the Silent Listener to Every Conversation.

The seven books, including the one he is reading, appear to be secular, although the one beside his hat on the bureau may be about the New Testament.

The Bible, probably quite large and old, is surely somewhere nearby, frequently opened and read, perhaps aloud.

But there are also these other books, and they matter, too.

The two kerosene lamps provide night-time light enough for peaceful reading, and the steel-rimmed glasses focus a page to clarity and wonder.

The nation has twenty thousand or more Postmasters, dealing in letters and stamps and the mail, which is also a form of religion, the Head of the House, the Unseen Guest, the Silent Listener.

It's a good life.

The going is slow and easy, a man has time enough in which to grow old.

When they put a slouching man into a statue of stone or steel standing all alone on a marble box in a place something like a courthouse, a school, a museum, or a church, anybody who goes there wants to know who the man is and why they put him up there.

The little girl is probably wondering what he's smiling about.

Well, his name was Will Rogers, he was part-Indian, born in Ardmore, Oklahoma, he wandered away to New York and fell to doing a rather unlikely kind of vaudeville act for Florenz Ziegfeld in an annual show called the Follies.

He was a rope-throwing, gum-chewing cowboy who made wisecracks about people and events in the daily news.

He sounded like a hired hand who might be passing the time of day with other lazy workers in the corral, but what he began to say in the 1920s about Presidents, Senators, and politicians in general was so casually critical and good-humoredly sarcastic that soon his remarks were daily news themselves.

He said simple things that seemed both truthful and outrageous, but not even the people he criticized minded especially because, true to the tradition of the West, he smiled as he knifed, and then pointed out that all he knew was what he read in the newspapers.

Part of an era that was openly frivolous and secretly corrupt, he was the first of a whole school of stand-up comedians who talked homely editorials on the state of the nation, and poked fun at the pretenses of power and wealth.

At his worst he was cute, at his best he was a plain man with cheek and the gift of gab.

Plenty, what lovely plenitude, what sweet peace and productivity, how near perfection are the grazing milk cows in the pasture beyond the cool stream, how near childhood's own heaven is the little girl in the white dress holding the calf, and her little brother holding a bouquet of wildflowers, in Wisconsin, sweet land of milk, butter, cheese, apples, and watermelons.

A calf to these kids is another child, another entity, another member of the family, with his own nature and personality, his own wishes and ideas about where to go for lunch or a look at what's happening.

What luck, what good luck it is to be part of Wisconsin.
May there always be such farms and such kids to pass their childhood in them.

Notice the grass, please.

Notice the earth, the table upon which the fine boy and the fine bull stand.

That earth is home, Texas, Oklahoma, New Mexico, Arizona, Utah, or Idaho.

The bull is a Black Angus, majestic, mighty, and worth a lot of money.

The boy is healthy, handsome, intelligent, and lucky.

(To be who he is and where he is.)

He is also a member of one of the greatest clubs in the world—certainly one of the few with a real excuse for being: the 4-H.

This is a club joined by the sons and daughters of farmers of all kinds who compete in the raising of crops of all kinds, including beef, lamb, wool, poultry, eggs, milk, butter, anything animal or vegetable that grows and is desirable.

The small farmer is being driven from the land by the tough competition of the great syndicates, and in some parts of the country by the rising costs of labor.

The syndicates can meet the demands of belatedly organized farm labor very easily, in spite of their crying, lying, and buying.

The small farmer can't pay hired hands a dollar-and-half an hour, two dollars an hour, and later on three dollars an hour, because if he did he wouldn't have any money left at the end of the year with which to pay the interest on his mortgage, get his farm machinery repaired, and buy seed.

Only rich men will remain small farmers, so their sons and daughters can know the beauty of that life.

The syndicates will produce greater crops at less expense than ever, in spite of farm labor at last being paid almost as much as it deserves.

What do the four H's stand for?

Home, hearth, health, happiness?

Head, heart, hand, hard-work?

Hope, hustle, harvest, hallelujah?

Any boy who can help a delicate little bull-calf grow into a monument of flawless physical truth has got to understand his own probable potential and truth, and therefore enjoy life fully.

The fattest, clumsiest, slowest boys, when asked what they want to be when they grow up by somebody like the television smilers who have become multi-millionaires making people and children behave like apes, reply, "Brain surgeon."

But once a boy on television actually said he wanted to be a veterinarian.

This astonished the smiling fraud, who asked the boy why.

"I like animals," the boy said.

The fact is that being a good animal doctor has got to be a more difficult and more fascinating profession than being a people doctor.

The variety of animals is great, although the basic patients are cats, dogs, cows, and horses.

Still, even elephants, boa constrictors, giraffes, lions, bears, and whales get sick and must either be healed or helped to die.

Imagine looking after a kangaroo with a stomachache.

A veterinarian and several assistants, students, apprentices, or amateurs are at work on a horse with a dental problem.

Perhaps the horse has other problems, too, but now it seems that a bad tooth is being extracted.

One is fascinated by the setting, the bed or table upon which the animal is carefully held fast, the bottles and instruments on the metal push-wagon—all to the end that the animal will not suffer undue pain and will be swiftly relieved of the offending member, or condition.

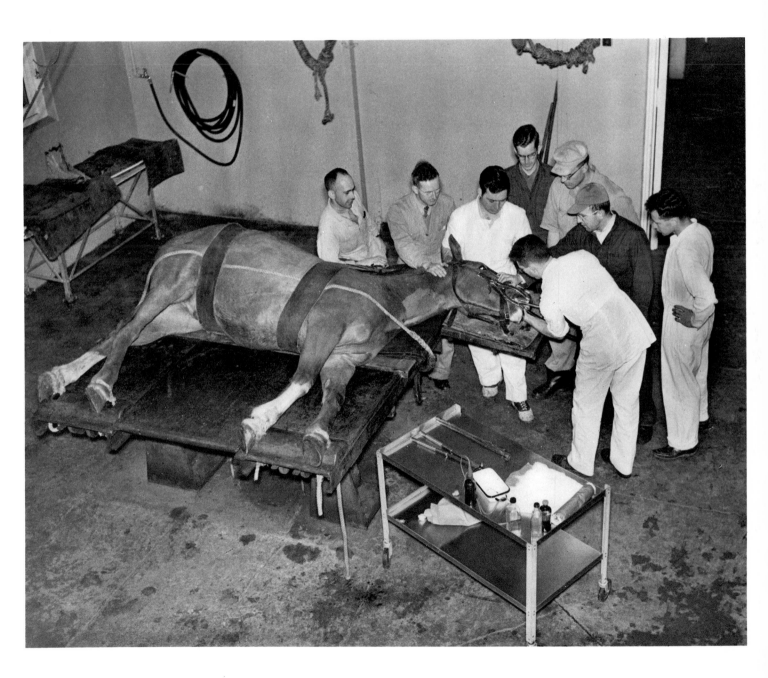

The rabbit, especially the great-big snow-white super-soft long-eared pink-eyed rabbit is the Ambassador from the Animal World to the World of Children, who are enchanted by the whole mystique of the living ball of patient timid mouth-quivering softness.

There is something of the secret ego of every child in the whole image and meaning of the rabbit: soft, delicate, white, vulnerable, longing-for-love, and scared to death but hopeful.

Kids reach out to such things—to pass along and to receive a transference of love, but sometimes even a rabbit will reject the gesture or misinterpret it and feign an attack (with teeth?) or hop away as far as there is to go.

But after a while they understand one another, they relax, the rabbit understands his goose is not cooked, and the child understands there is a way to reach out to love—let the hand hold something the rabbit likes to eat.

And voilà, there's the beginning of a friendship.

The face of the small boy beyond the mesh-wire is the face of childhood's own all-time wonder about the infinite variety of things in the world.

Now, here's this great big living snowball.

What does it mean?

It's got to mean something, doesn't it?

And so it is with everything else he sees, either for the first time or again and again: it has got to mean something, doesn't it?

But soon enough he stops even asking, and lets it go, because there's just too much of everything.

126

Four Cub Scouts in uniform with one Leader in uniform and one Den Mother
in uniform—in Texas, but it could be in any of the other states, including Alaska, the
Hawaiian Islands, Puerto Rico, the Virgin Islands, Wake, Guam, or wherever else the
American influence goes.

Little soldiers?

Is that what it comes to?

Yes, that is precisely what it comes to, and that is the foolishness of it.

Forget the uniforms, forget the leader in his military uniform, forget the Den Mother in
her uniform, and if small boys must be herded together for the good of their souls,
then just take them to interesting places and let them have their own idea of a little fun—
not any adult's idea.

A certain amount of uniformity is inevitable in any case—there is no need to put
small boys (and their sisters who very early are initiated into the Brownies, and then into
the Girl Scouts) into actual uniforms, which invariably suggest soldiers, and encourage all
of the unfortunate preoccupations of soldiering.

But it's fun, it's all right, it's harmless, it's really great training for the little fellows.
Jesus was a Cub, so was Moses, so was Mohammed, so was Walt Whitman, Mark
Twain, Eugene O'Neill, William Faulkner, and Ezra Pound.

Flowing rivers overflow, and when they do there is a little too much of a good thing, a delight at first to kids who need and cherish change and surprise, and then no longer a delight but a danger, the rolling water surrounding the house and then coming to the front steps, on up the steps to the door, into the house, across all of the floors, lifting and floating chairs and tables.

The great Mississippi River, the Old Man of the rivers of America, every now and then is sent more water than its old roadways can send south easily to the Gulf of Mexico.

It happens to all rivers.

Living there is the risk taken by people who need the sense and solace of rivers.

We can telephone for help, and get away with our skins, at any rate, but what about the animals, looking at us?

This is their place, too, what about the animals?

Jesus H. Christ, is the government never going to know how to keep the Mississippi from going on a rampage?

Must a farmer first of all teach his kids to swim, and build his barns with escape towers for the animals to climb to.

Must he keep a boat in his garage for the inevitable flood, and his safe get-away?

The water everywhere makes a beautiful if awesome picture, but we're farmers, not fish.

Let's flood the White House and see how they like it.

Sending the Vice President, the Red Cross, the Salvation Army, and groups of well-behaved convicts after the flood helps a little, but not really, it doesn't stop the next flood.

Language is an incredible thing, a preposterous thing, an angelic thing.

It is unbelievable in its beauty, variety, and usage.

Man's language, not the language of geese, which is also beautiful, but something else again.

The spoken language of man, in all its variations, is a choir singing hosanna to something.

The written language of man is a long sweet sorrowful and joyous prayer.

How language fell into the mouth of man, and then moved from sounds to marks and settled in the mind and spirit is the great story—and then all of a sudden there is another language: a language of mathematics, numbers, symbols, weights, measures, speeds, probabilities, pressures, apportionings, reservations, withdrawals, cancellations, reappearances, reflections, banishments, restorations, pneumatics—all to the end that something will be understood, something more will be discovered, identified, and put to work.

The multiplication table is as far as I got, and my taxes show it.

I still don't know how to come out even a little ahead.

Where's my Rolls Royce?

Where's my alligator shoes?

Where's my $300 suits?

Where's my house in Acapulco?

Where's my real estate?

Where's my pretty girls looking for gifts?

Where's my power?

Where?

Where *would* they be?

Nowhere.

I didn't learn arithmetic.

I got left back.

When they told me, Learn arithmetic, I laughed at them, but how right they were—my own illiterate old people with their instinct for what's useful and what ain't.

Ah, well, you can't have everything.

If you can understand a poem, why should you imagine you ought to be able also to

understand a tax law?

Books.

What wonders they are.

A library.

What an incredible place it is.

Youth, expectancy, anger, revolution, destruction, reformation, reconstruction—almost everything starts in the Public Library.

This beautiful picture reminds me of where I spent so much of my time from 1916 to 1926 in Fresno: in the old red-brick Public Library on Broadway across the street from the White Theatre.

The upper racks of books were marked Philosophy, Theosophy, Geography, History, Biography, Grapes, and Raisins.

The variety, age, and neglect of the books depressed and delighted me, by turns.

It didn't occur to me until sometime in 1928 when I first went to New York that not everything in every book is holy writ, a lot of it is stuff that only rhymes with it, and it is frequently written by absolutely honest and talented men—just a little stupid on a grand scale, that's all, the same as writers now.

Fresno demolished the old library, and put up a magnificent new one.

That's fine, but why knock down the old one and throw away its beautiful garbage books?

Now it's an empty parking lot.

The White Theatre has been demolished, too.

One of the most beautiful theatres in the world.

The old Court House was brought down, too—after three years of hard work on the part of Vagim to save it.

Vagim?

That's right.

Ed Vagim put up a good fight, but in the end the wreckers knocked down the old Court House, too.

Looking at people is perhaps the greatest of the simple pleasures.

The fascination lies in the fact that people are all alike and yet every person is unique.

The measurable differences between a woman considered plain and one considered beautiful are not great, but in people only a very little difference makes a very great difference.

People watching something are worth watching, and they are frequently even more interesting than the thing they are watching.

Watching a parade is a city sport to which no admission is charged.

Parades in America are divided into categories—patriotic, like Armistice Day; personality, like Lindbergh in New York; political, like Bobby-Determined-to-be-Both-President-and-Great (but not too likely to be the first and beyond the second).

There are other kinds of parades, the most famous of which is the Circus, unfortunately no longer an annual event in every city and town in the country.

Funeral parades are beautiful, especially in southern cities and towns where jazz is played on the way to the graveyard.

The Thanksgiving Day parade in New York is something new, invented by Macy's to stimulate fresh buying.

These are working people, and their kids.

They wear plain clothes.

Every adult has long since given up any hope of being a movie star, marrying money, or making it to the moon.

Who are the people looking at?

The Unknown Soldier, Lindbergh, Bobby, Macy, a corpse?

No.

They're looking at Santa Claus, that's who.

(Made out of snow, hard candy, oranges, fire, and crazy kindness, the indestructible fat boy of love himself.)

136

There's something here, along the lines of determination, dignity, and hilarity that calls for either careful consideration or instant dismissal.

United Electrical Radio & Machine Workers of America.

UE Local 501 C. I. O. AUX.

Buffalo New York.

All neatly printed on the hide of the drum: worn and held by the lady in the costume.

Directly ahead is the lady with the clashing cymbals.

And just beyond the big drum we can see the upper part of the head of another member of the AUX.

Careful consideration tells one to be respectful of these musical ladies, but somehow it can't be done.

They are delightful, no doubt about that.

One really loves them, but one can't quite get over the hats and the feminine mystique.

The trouble with Buffalo is that it isn't Hollywood, and the trouble with being in the AUX. is that it isn't the same as being in a movie that might earn you an Oscar nomination.

What it isn't is fair.

The sun is strong, the bees are drunk with light and color.

At Harvard, Yale, Princeton, Dartmouth, or Cornell all of a sudden studying must be postponed, and so it is: the students are out on the grass under the trees, some in the shade, some in the light, to half-listen to a band concert.

There's stuff from the Vienna Woods, from along the Danube, and from the Opera Ball—what does it mean, a hundred years later and six thousand miles away?

And yet it continues to be the very substance of our memory and longing, even though we know the music is poor and the influence absurd.

That was a time of ignorance, innocence, and romance.

This is a time of intelligence, loneliness, and truth.

Music out of doors, music in the streets, made by inferior musicians, is sometimes the greatest music of all—for being where it is, away from the opera house or concert hall and its ladies and gentlemen.

Away from the high finance of culture for everybody—which is always only culture for the same people, God love them.

Any city that prevents music in the streets is a dying city.

Streets are also for passing celebrators, as well as for slaves.

This photograph is a work of art.

It is not necessary for photographs to be works of art, it is enough for them to see something and to hold fast to a moment of truth, or to an aspect of a moment of truth.

Most photographs report.

They add something to the record, for reference.

This photograph is art because the photographer saw (or made, if you like) a composition, a relationship in a number of objects in themselves beautifully wrought, and he captured the art of it in the nick of time.

Had the occupant of Room 3 at the Hotel de Paris in Georgetown, Colorado, come in and taken his key from place 5 on the rack the picture would not be complete.

Such hotels will soon be gone forever, in favor of Holiday Inns everywhere, and then somebody very rich will build a whole antique hotel with everything in it the way things were a hundred years ago, and only very rich people will be able to go there.

142

Physical effort is beautiful to behold, especially when it's overambitious, as in this young clam-digger.

He's dug too many to carry, but he's giving it a good try.

The strain of his effort has transformed his flawless face into a delightful but grotesque mask of a kind one sometimes sees in exhibitions of the art of Africa and certain Pacific Islands, although this boy's Island is only Long, where the good clams are.

The fun of clam-digging is that clams are there, although you've got to learn the trick of knowing where to dig for them, and sometimes you make a strike, so that getting a pail full is a matter of only half an hour.

Also, clams are living things, living inside their clever shells, which sometimes have designs similar to those in Indian baskets and blankets, but of course the Indians got the designs from the clams, not the other way around.

Furthermore, clams are food, and very good food, too.

A feast of steamed clams with their hot juice is as good for the soul as it is for the body.

And white and red clam chowder is one of the truly great American dishes: Coney Island red, New England white.

It's great to go clamming, that's all.

The way it is said to have happened is that he wanted the Democratic nomination but found the Kennedy machine too much for him—he was rich, too, but not all that rich.

He didn't like the family from Boston.

He wasn't interested in being nominated for Vice President.

As a gesture, John offered him the office, certain that he would not accept.

But he did accept.

The painful days of being stupid Vice President dragged on and on, and then in Dallas, not far from his own great home and holdings, it happened.

On the President's airplane about to take off for Washington, he raised his arm in the taking of the oath of office.

And then he was what he wanted to be in the first place.

President.

There was about a year to election time.

There was the brother shooting off his mouth all the time, with his Donald Duck voice.

There was work to do.

He ran the show at the convention of the Democratic Party in Atlantic City, chose Hubert Humphrey instead of Bobby as his running mate, and clobbered the Republican candidate, Barry Goldwater.

On television his face turned thuggish, his voice grew mean and hard, as if he were a Texas gangster, even though his words affected holiness, love of democracy, concern about the prevention of pain, illness, violence, and death among people everywhere.

Nobody—nobody—not even his mother, his father, his brother, his sister, his wife, his daughters, his best friends, his cabinet—told him how to be a great President.

He figured it out for himself, but as he was not a great man in the first place, it didn't work.

All he needed to do was get out of Vietnam until their civil war had been concluded, and then if they wanted his help, to give it insofar as he was able to.

146

Here's Adam, here's Eve.

Here's Cain, here's Abel, and their brothers and sisters, in the Garden of Eden, shifted just an edge from far away in dreamland to precisely here, underfoot, in Gee's Bend, Alabama.

There's the tree, and the snake's in that burlap sack where he damn well belongs, by now—there is such a thing as pausing a moment to catch the breath, look around, count the kids, and try to remember their names, isn't there?

They are all beautiful, Adam, Eve, and every one of the kids.

But the whole world is jumping up and down hollering at the fruitful to stop being fruitful, begging them to be sophisticated, worldly, and swave, as the comics put it, but the world is full of poor people and they don't know how to be swave.

But it isn't only poor people who believe in the future, a lot of rich people do, too.

Prizefighters, Presidents, politicians, baseball players, senators, track stars, bankers, delinquents, valedictory speech-makers, dope pushers, professors, civil rights marchers, millionaires, rioters, windbags, you got to have them all to make a world and a human family.

The rich and superior are the first to say they are the same as the poor and inferior—and to stand by what they say, too, because it doesn't cost anything, doesn't mean anything, but does sound good.

(We've got to do something about Watts.

Good thinking, how about inventing the tea-kettle?)

The Holy Family, that's what it is.
They don't believe.
They are.
They don't talk.
They move.
They don't promise.
They wait.
They don't plan.
They grow.
They don't understand.
They live.
What the hell does anybody else do?

148

The beautiful bell of liberty, forever.

In Philadelphia, heard one morning when oppression ended and something else began. (Or so we say.)

Poor Richard heard the ringing of the bell and wrote something new for the Almanac.

But if this is a liberty bell, a bell to proclaim freedom for all, what are the other bells and what do they proclaim?

The telephone bell, for instance, what does its rude nagging ring proclaim?

Why do people who call long distance believe the distance involved justifies the intrusion?

Church bells are a joy, pure and simple, and whether they proclaim liberty or forfeiture of it doesn't matter.

Fire engine bells have a kind of charm, but sirens drown them out.

Locomotives hardly ever toll their bells any more.

Strings of camel bells, all muted and flat in tone, can be bought and hung about in a house.

Anybody with a tribal memory of caravans will find them a special pleasure, like my father's kid brother who had to have six or seven strings of them in his house, so that brushing upon them he could be restored in spirit to the peace of the great eastern spaces and to the slow pace of the camels—they never hurried but always got there.

Liberty?

Freedom?

There are no bells that toll for such elusive abstractions.

All kinds of people have been photographed for about one hundred years, but never so extensively—democratically—as during the past fifty years, in still pictures, in moving pictures, and in television pictures.

Almost nobody comes along who is not photographed, whose picture does not appear somewhere, at least in a family album.

Crowds of all kinds, however, continue to be anonymous, or at best identified only broadly: Construction Workers, T.V.A. Dam, a hundred or more faces of workingmen.

Well, a face is a face, and every face tells a little of the story of the man to whom it belongs.

The faces of men who do hard work are also unmistakably the faces of poets, comedians, saints, philosophers, inventors, sons, brothers, and fathers.

A face in a photograph is no more than a flash of its total reality, which is in constant motion from birth to death.

The flash held fast by the camera in these faces is a flash of comparative youth, health, intelligence, confidence, easy pride, humor, and faith—but faith in what?

God, country, family, union, industry, engineering, or what?

Surely in all of these things, but mostly in the future.

The kids of these workers constitute a far larger invisible crowd on their way to a far greater variety of destinations.

These workers have their jobs, and in these jobs they are simultaneously liberated and held prisoner, but their kids are at home, waiting their turn to go into action.

Most of them are smiling.

All of them are thinking.

Work, any kind of work, gives the human visage dignity.

Idleness imposes upon it a mask of impending mischief, or crime.

It is better (for the man himself) to work for ten dollars a day than to hope for a fortune, free of charge.

What we have here is almost unbelievable, on several accounts: this young woman fishing in the surf is pretty, she isn't kidding around about fishing, she means business, she's rigged out to catch fish, and it seems that she's actually caught one and is netting it.

What is it about fetching a fish?

Why is it so deeply satisfying in a way that nothing else is?

Consider the shape and design of a fish.

It is a flawless thing—the very design from which has come the submarine, the small boat, the yacht, the great ship, as well as all forms of the flying machine, especially as it develops and improves.

Fishing has appealed to many complex souls, including a number of Presidents, especially Herbert Hoover.

Simpler (or supposedly simpler) souls, like Huck Finn, for instance, loved fishing not only for the hunger the caught fish satisfied but for the loafing that was inseparable from the catching of them.

It also meant being free, in every sense: from Pap (the incompetent father), from school, from the family, from all tedious responsibility to somebody or something.

Those who fish have a good strong introspective side.

They need to be out of schedules, and pressures—and fishing carries them to timelessness.

(Instantly.)

The early Christians who were despised, ridiculed, hounded, persecuted, and punished used the sign of the fish for identification.

The sea is vast, almost three times as vast as the land, and its depths and topography are still hidden and unknown, and it is in the water, and in its depths that the fish come into and go out of being.

By the billions, incessantly, endlessly, infinitely.

It isn't necessary for us to believe that we are all fish, but in a sense, in an interior sense, it is true.

Thirteen women and a little girl, sitting on a trailer at a picnic in Kansas.
The women are the wives of organized farm workers.
For years they have been earnestly involved in the hard work of making good homes for their husbands and kids.

Each of these faces deserves long study.
Each tells a rather wonderful story—of patience, faith, intelligence and humor.

These women are beautiful, every one of them.
That is the important thing about them.

There's this thing in the world called ice cream, and it takes its place early in anybody's life as one of the best of the better things—to have, to eat, to remember, to long for, to know is there.

Chocolate-coated ice cream on a stick is very good, although now and then the ice cream inside gets gooey.

This doesn't allow a person of four, or five, or six to take his time eating the stuff.

The big girl here is trying to understand what's going on, and the little girl is offering her a paper napkin.

We just bought these, why are they falling to pieces in our hands?

The ice cream man knows perfectly well what's happening, and why, but isn't telling.

Kids might as well learn that even ice cream isn't absolutely dependable, or as Wallace Stevens put it in a poem that is famous among poets: "The only emperor is the emperor of ice cream."

In short, the only supreme thing is change: ice cream melts.

(Sometimes prematurely, as here.)

The noble boxer is thinking about the whole thing in all of its dimensions:—ah sun, ah world, ah friends, O little girls, O time, O shadows, O ice cream.

O yes, look at me, but don't forget that I look at you, too.

What do you see, what do you see?

An old Indian woman with a wrinkled face?

A girl, the Chief's daughter, Princess Prairie Dog, a mother, an ignorant woman, Lady Wildflower, illiterate, inarticulate, the bride of Wild Horse Harry, superstitious?

See what you like, it's all true, but let me tell you in your own language that what I see are abandoned old Chevrolets and Fords rusting in the hot plains where not so long ago I saw decent animals.

And I see you of course.

Let me say that again, not so much for emphasis as for simplicity.

I see you.

Do you, ever?

What we did is move, and then some more, and then again, and after that we moved again, and then we looked around and moved again, and then we thought it might be better if we moved, so we moved again, and that's what we did.

The only animals that moved with us were the half-starved horses and dogs.

Can you tell what I'm thinking?

I can't.

I know what I'm thinking but I can't tell you.

It really isn't too much to tell, if anything it's too little.

But maybe I ought to try, maybe I ought to try a little.

We don't understand.

We are.

The sun is something important to us.

We trust in the sun.

We have excellent relations with the sun.

Well, I can't tell you.

I can, but it doesn't come out the way it is with us.

No. 30 has a job to do, ladies and gentlemen, boys and girls, on the beach at Atlantic City, in the good old summertime.

Anybody drowning in the surf can expect No. 30 to run out there and save his life, because he is a Lifeguard.

At the same time he is a member of the Beach Patrol, as the badge on his cap testifies.

Around his neck hangs a whistle, which means that in the event of major crime he can whistle for help, as cops on city streets do.

But what might the crimes on the beach ever be?

Hugging and kissing on an Army blanket?

Yes, there is a law against it, and No. 30 knows its number and wording.

As he separates the lawbreakers, the sunbathers all around smile, they don't boo.

Privacy is privacy only if it's in private.

Privacy in public can bring up a lot of little kids who say, "Go ahead, we only want to watch, we won't tell anybody."

Rolling down the roller coaster is a break for kids who are not permitted to go to a bar and get drunk.

Paying a dime, fifteen cents, or perhaps a quarter to ride the roller coaster at an amusement park is to shake up the lethargy of the soul, to get the jammed kaleidoscope of the mind jarred loose, so that new pictures can be permitted to happen in it, as they will and must.

A crazy ride that takes no more than two minutes banishes boredom, despair, indifference, staleness, and hopelessness from the heart of a child.

Why?

Because the travel makes no sense, starts nowhere, arrives nowhere, but the passenger on that railroad has been to the moon, traveling a course fraught with disaster, and then he has come safely home.

Sensible adults take the trip too, but not the giants of the adult world.

They never take a ride on a roller coaster, not even to patronize a great American invention, in which the Americans lead the Russians by a good half a century.

Americans have gotten married everywhere and under all circumstances, but I don't remember anybody ever having been married on a roller coaster.

This seems odd, since the allegorical possibilities are so obvious.

People are forever looking for a reason and a right to shout, howl, scream, and screech.

They get what they are looking for when they get on the roller coaster.

It helped long before free psychiatric clinics were established.

Snow is the most useful by-product of the weather, for exploitation on behalf of fun by kids and lighthearted adults.

Walking through a heavy fall of snow gives the face a benediction of ghostly cold kisses.

Beholding the white of snow upon everything after a night of silent falling is one of the most satisfying of the simple pleasures.

Making and throwing snowballs is calisthenics for the muscle-bound soul, and an instant cure for everything.

Helping kids to make a snowman is being a great sculptor, but what about the snowman himself?

What about him?

Well, he appears to be nothing but a mass of shaped snow, but to the kid who made him the snowman is himself, heroic and melting.

These two warm and laughing snowboys are enjoying Snow Usage Number One: snow in the making of a snowman.

The wonder of it all is that the most popular religions of the world originated in hot countries—rocky, sandy, dry, and glaring.

Christianity dragged snow into the act, but only far from where it started.

It isn't that snow is holier than sand, it's just that it comes down from above, covers everything, is white, cold, silent, and stays put long enough at least for the beginning of love, and a prayer or two.

Going to the cemetery, going to the grave of a member of the family, or to the grave of a friend, or to the grave of a great man, is an interesting custom that's easy to understand and to be respectful of, although nobody is there, absolutely nobody at all, and surely a better place to pay homage to anyone gone is where he had flourished.

A man is not his lifeless bones in the ground, he is a ghost in the living world, being among his fellows as he had been while he ran his line to the end.

Having left the world, having left himself, there is no further need for a man to be concerned about material things.

If while he lived he believed somebody or something somewhere else might be impressed by something about himself or by his behavior in the world, it is too late to make an impression the minute he's dead.

Everybody is somebody, dead or alive, to somebody, that's what it comes to.

Many come and go in the equivalent of secrecy—these alone compel profound mourning.

The others were known and experienced, and when they are mourned the mourners are actually mourning themselves, but of course that's all right, too.

Joe, Mary, we're standing here because the line's running out for us, too, and confidentially this isn't exactly the best place in the world for the line to end.

Didn't we have in mind fields in light with streams lazing through them and all bodies young and easy and breathing?

Ah, well, we didn't make the world or life, we just found ourselves there, living it, the same as everybody else.

168   Be seeing you.

A sack race for secretaries is being won by the dean of secretaries, as of course all sack races at picnics should be won.

She is the oldest, she always means business, no hanky-panky or jiggery-pokery, she knows what to do, and how and when to do it, she doesn't throw her weight around in brightly-colored soft wool sweaters, she makes her boss feel like Alexander the Great, and she can hop forward in a sack faster than the boss's wife can *walk*.

But the losers are the charmers, they're the ones all of us non-executives love, especially the one who's falling flat on her laughing face.

Of course the audience believes that what is going on is a sack race.
Sure it is.

A Sergeant in the Army of the United States who has been trained to drive a tank rests for a moment outside his tank after he has driven it through mud and water, as part of his training for war.

A tank is a ridiculous piece of machinery, no matter how you look at it, or try to justify it.

The purpose of a tank is to go where nothing else can go and to destroy whatever is there, including soldiers.

Tanks are a form of tractor, harvesting, or threshing machine: the difference is a tank is designed solely to deal in death and destruction.

172   Any man connected with a tank has to stop and think about it now and then.

When D. H. Lawrence wrote in a novel about reporting to his London draft board during World War I, ten years later he was still hot about his sense of outrage at being ordered to get out of his clothes, so that he might be thoroughly examined.

But five million or more American boys and men obeyed orders without protest, and still do, most likely because the draft was what was happening, and in any case a protest would only mean even more trouble.

When a very serious accident is happening and no blood has been shed, it is a good idea to leave well enough alone, on the chance that the accident won't end in murder.

Once you start to protest, you can't stop, so don't start, because it has got to cost you either your life or your mind.

Not long after World War I almost every man in public life insisted that the next war would be fought only by those who start it, by the leaders, as they're called, by the owners, by the profit-makers.

And so of course there would be no war, they said.

But even while they were speaking the war was happening.

All wars start in times of peace, in reasonable, articulate, sensible men, who simply don't know they are totally helpless.

If there is, then, a conspiracy, who are the conspirators?

The sad but probably scientific answer, or at any rate the probably truthful answer, is that there is no conspiracy, and there are no conspirators among men.

For centuries the Arabs, Greeks, and Romans didn't speak of Fate for nothing.

Their experience instructed them to put it that way.

Our ambition impels us to believe in Control, but so far control has been a fantasy.

174   **L**isten carefully to the Sergeant, boys, he may just have the answer.

Big brother or older boy helping little brother or younger boy to learn to ride a bike, both of them barefooted on an unpaved road in front of an old house with a carefully neglected lawn of weeds and little wildflowers, that's living, man.

The old lawn-mower is abandoned, as this is no time to fool around at work, this is a time to live, to ride, to go, to be ready for the getaway one of these days, get on my bike and ride from the old house and the old gang in the old neighborhood to the stage in New York, in the death-defying act of a boy only eight years old riding a bicycle with only one hand.

The bicycle is the greatest transportation machine of them all.

The design of the thing from its earliest forms to its latest is a wonder, and the manufacturers haven't stopped yet.

Many a bike has taken off into space and landed safely on the moon, unbeknownst to science, history, television, or the news services: a bike has a good place to sit, a place to hold on at high speed, and a pumping place for the feet, how much more science and invention does a small boy need?

But the bicycle has always been a joke, too: one of the greatest vaudeville acts involved a tramp-clown on a bike that went to pieces as he tried to ride it.

And other clowns have ridden bikes only twelve inches in height.

Statesmen never go to their work on bicycles.

176   Perhaps they ought to try it, though.

This place has a spittoon, a wall telephone, two card players with new cigars in their mouths, one kibitzer wearing a white belt, three sporting photographs in frames on the wall, and a high shelf of something that looks like a lot of horns of some kind, so where are we?

And what's going on?

We're out west in Carson City, Nevada, and this is a game of cribbage in the fire house, that's all.

Fires don't happen every other hour, so of course there is a lot of time to use up, waiting, and a man can't be forever studying something by correspondence while he's waiting.

A time comes when a fireman decides he no longer wants to be something else, all he wants to do is move from one day to the next, and let the alarms come in as they must.

Cézanne's painting of The Card Players happens ten million times a day all over the world, in ten million variations.

This is one, American style, Far West.

The idea is to have a contest going that isn't quite a matter of life and death, and yet has all the potentials of that contest, and all of its fascination and drama.

Certain ornery horses of America make a lifetime career of not getting the idea that a horse is a horse and must behave like one and permit himself to be ridden.

Such horses can be exhausted into not being able to buck any more, but the next day when a cowboy tries to ride them they go berserk all over again.

Well, what *about* horses?

What about the business of breaking them?

Is it the only way to make a horse useful?

No, there is another school that follows a procedure of kindness, patience, and affection, but it takes a lot of time.

Does breaking a horse harm it?

Only in a way that is desirable to men.

The world itself is a kind of rodeo at which sooner or later men are broken and trained to be, variously, adults, citizens, husbands, wage-earners, slaves, bill-payers, consumers, voters, law-abiders, lawn-cutters, insurance-takers, pill-takers, fathers, cigarette-smokers, television-watchers, and all of the other highly organized things a nation needs by the millions in order to collect a lot of taxes and protect a lot of freedom all over the world which everybody would be very grateful if outsiders would just leave alone.

Look here.

Look at just an inch of Montana, at a sheepherder's wheeled house and hearth.

What address is this?

Large, unfenced, alone, and apart.

In all probability this easy visitor of the least visited places of the West is a Basque, born in the Pyrenees, and brought over to do a job no one else can do, or wants to do: for three years, or four, or five, for the good money of it, to take home.

If he decides to stay, sending for a Basque girl, who bears him sons, born in Montana, Idaho, Nevada, Arizona, or California, these sons will not become sheepherders, and one of them might just become the governor of his state.

Laxalt of Nevada, for instance, whose brother is a writer.

If you want to know the earth you have got to be willing to spend a lot of time with it.

Racing across it on a super-highway won't do it.

The remote places of the earth speak to the visitor in a language almost as difficult as Basque itself, which even philological experts continue to puzzle over.

The language may even be without words or symbols, having its being in grass, rocks, streams, and predators.

A lot of people, men and women, are sitting and standing somewhere, some looking to the right, some to the left.

Where are we?

What's going on?

Is it a revival meeting, by Billy Graham?

It could be, but it isn't.

A public affairs meeting?

Out of the question.

Such a meeting would attract very few people.

A political rally?

Possibly.

But that isn't what it is.

These are a few of the people who paid anywhere from ten to fifty dollars each to get into the Astrodome in Houston, Texas, to see a prizefight.

Going to a prizefight does a number of useful things to their psyches: releases their aggressions, hatreds, fears, anxieties, and a lot of other things of that kind.

They get excited, their muscles get taut, they jump and holler, and they aren't really who they seem to be most of the time.

The prizefight business is big business on account of these wonderful, unpsychoanalyzed, unpsychoanalyzable people.

Great numbers of people, every one of them alive, and damned glad to be, but awfully confused about what it's for.

Nobody is able to see things as a camera may be made to see them.

Even if you were to lie flat on your back in Rockefeller Plaza and look straight up, you would not see what the camera has here seen.

There would be no encirclement, no drawing-in of the skyscrapers, no tight design.

Not even in troubled sleep, not even in a nightmare, does the interior eye, the eye of memory, see the city as the camera here sees it.

What counts is not the height and weight of the great buildings, it's the patch of sky beyond them, and the white clouds, as if noticed for the first time by a millionaire in a casket, or by a beggar half-asleep on a patch of lawn wasting another day during which he could be out making his fame and fortune.

The sky and the clouds are the millionaire's requiem and the beggar's justification.

Hell below, heaven above, they are partners who long ago stopped speaking to one another, hell because his partner is a dreamer, heaven because his partner is a fool.

The fulfillment of a poor boy's dream is the building of his own house, not his father's house, or the house of another poor boy who got rich.

His very own house, designed by a timid and needy architect, or why would he take so much fantastic stuff and put timber and glass and paint to it?

Or a clever architect, eager to earn money and win the admiration of a rich man.

But more likely a sincere hard-working architect who didn't believe for one moment that the house he had designed was simple, silent, solid lunacy—such as this house in Eugene, Oregon.

A rich man did that, and let it be a lesson to you.

Houses are meant to do something for their owners that perhaps their faces and figures aren't able to do—make a desirable impression, for instance: "Let the world see the real texture of my spirit: I am a poet, not a pickpocket."

This house is a poem, a piece of wedding cake, a song, a sign, a statement, a donation of a large sum of money for the rehabilitation of bats with aspirations to be butterflies, a joke, a groan of anguish, a roar of laughter.

No man need feel embarrassed about entering such a house, but to leave it in broad daylight is possible only by a man who has been blind from birth.

Even so, such a house is a work of art, and should not be molested.

On the contrary, it should be kept in good repair, so that poor people may see for themselves the terrible price a man must pay for being rich.

This is the house that money built, no doubt about that.

A hundred years ago the poor boy who got rich spent about twenty thousand dollars to build the house.

Was he gypped?

Yes, but not nearly as badly as you and I were yesterday, and our houses cost twice as much and can't even smile, let alone laugh.

Out West in the Indian world there are these incredible apartment houses, out in the land of space, up against great rocks and cliffs the Indians long ago put up a whole series of connected dwellings which together form one magnificent edifice.

What might it have been that sent them from the great open spaces to little rooms up against great rocks?

Fear?

A place of peace and security in which to pursue the crafts of weaving and pottery, from which to go hunting whenever necessary?

Or was it need to build, to use the materials at hand in the making of something of their own that might rival some of nature's rock masses?

Culture starts when a house is built to stand forever, and even though it never does, because forever is just long enough to witness the crumbling of anything, the illusion of indestructibility serves the useful purpose of providing everybody with the time and the place in which to find out who he is and what he wants to do about it.

Let's get this approximately right, that was hard work for all of us, we don't want anything that's not coming to us, but we'd be awfully grateful to have every bit of what is, because let's face it, we can use every bit, and then some.

Rag padding on the knees or else the overalls wear through, and overalls cost money.

Cotton is white and soft, and it doesn't look at all like coins of money, but picking it, picking a whole lot of it, all of us together, the little girls getting the hang of it, is the only way we know how to have a perfect right to get some.

It's all by weight.

Nobody, nobody in God's green earth, is going to cheat us, we know that, we've always known it, but it's nice to see what our work comes to on the scale, we trust the plantation owner and his courteous and honest daughter, and we don't believe there is anything like a catch in the scale or in anything else, hardly, it's just that weighing-time is happy-time, resting-time, time to learn how much we're going to get in coins of money and to think about the wonderful things we are going to buy with it.

They're different, they're different, they're nice enough in their place, but they're different, more like animals, not like us, shiftless really, no ambition, if it was left to them daddy says, if we didn't give them easy work to do daddy says, if we didn't give them money daddy says, if we didn't give them homes to live in daddy says, if we weren't kind to them all the time daddy says—he says it all the time, he says it without saying anything, I've heard him say it every day all my life, I believe it with all my heart and soul, because there is no finer man than daddy and daddy's at his best when he's saying it.

Muhammad Ali is a superior American boy who happens to be a Negro, the heavyweight boxing champion of the world, a member in good standing of the political, religious and philosophical order of Black Muslims, an objector to personal participation in war, a payer of enormous taxes, a writer and reciter of amusing verse, a lover of little children, an effective extemporaneous public speaker, and a genius.

He has fought more times in one year than any other champion, and he has made a lot of worthy but second-and-third-rate fighters rich, many of them Negro, many of them not.

So far in the ring he has not yet once been hurt, dazed, frightened, confused, unaware, or not totally in command of the situation.

He has a very powerful mind and spirit in a superior body.

He knows only time will get him, as it finally gets all men.

In this fascinating photograph of five flashes of Muhammad in his fight in Houston with Ernie Terrell it isn't necessary to know who is who—it was the Muslim and not the Christian who won, but only against time, of course.

194

For kids Halloween is the greatest day of all, because witchcraft is in the air, piracy, blackmail, spooks, masks, costumes, excitement, and childhood needs these things.

What's the fun of always being expected to be good, of trying to do right, of caring about every lapse of manners?

One night a year a man aged nine and a woman aged eight and all of their friends become the most daring and devilish sides of themselves, and they raid the world for loot and love.

Trick or treat, give or lose, live or die, believe or suffer the consequences.

All performed, all in a pageant, all in a parade of pretense and a reversal of the balance of power.

The kids are the lords and ladies of the night-world of human experience for a couple of hours, demanding and getting payment for protection in the form of jelly beans, cookies, apples, and if they happen to be at the front door of their own house a quick kiss from a total stranger who might just be a boy's mother or a girl's father.

How about me in my father's derby?
How about me in the mask my mother wore at the country club ball?

What fun it is not to be yourself.
What fun it is to be free and bad, and proud of it.

The weather in Iowa hushes the landscape in the winter and keeps it lively the rest of the year.

Spring is all *aleap* with the new green of crops, weeds, and foliage.

Summer is all ripeness, heaviness, power, action, birds, beavers, dogs, cats, horses.

Fall is a time of smiling, looking around, remembering the hot days, getting ready for the end of the yellow, brown, golden, and red, and the arrival of the gray, white and black.

And then all of a sudden snow starts to fall and there it is, there's another year come and gone, the whole world covered in silent softness, all white.

This farmer has a pretty good house, big, ramshackle, old, spacious, but what he's really got is his great trees, all majestic in their winter nakedness and sleep.

Such trees mean shade, green, leafery, birds, sculpture, and music made by wind among the leaves and branches.

Farmers don't tend to be eloquent about such things, but I've seen a farmer go back to his farm ten years after he sold it just to look at the great trees he planted long long ago.

Is it all money, though?

All *for* money, with government allotments and guarantees and payoffs?

Of course it is.

So what?

Everything else is, too, including praying, why shouldn't the hard work of the man of the land also be for money?

The bright banners are spanning Main Street.

The pot-bellied cops have removed their jackets to keep cool as they keep the crowds in line.

Every uniform in every closet in every house has been brought out and again tried on for size.

The old fools who not so long ago were young fools have squeezed into the uniforms, to walk the streets again—to the same old music: "And the monkey wrapped his tail around the flagpole; my country it is of thee that I sing; keep the home fires burning; Madamoiselle from Armentières; I didn't raise my boy to be a Vice President; hello central give me no man's land; just a baby's prayer at twilight; pack up your troubles in an old kit bag and smile smile smile."

There are girls in the world, baton-twirlers some of them, with show biz in their bones.

That's why we win our wars.

Twirling batons in parades or at football games is a special American activity for healthy, pretty, lively girls, and some day soon when a woman is finally elected President, she may very well be a pretty girl from Indianapolis who was famous there long ago as a drum majorette.

Every girl has a right to be the star of some crazy show somewhere, what's the matter with the show on Armistice Day in the old hometown?

200

Something swift happens, frequently surprising, sometimes unbelievable, and all of a sudden a man who was himself only a moment ago a child finds himself romping with two small boys who are himself all over again: his son's sons, or his daughter's.

He sees himself in each of them: again his eyes are perfect, his hands, fingers and nails are all perfect, his laughter is new and joyous, and suddenly he's seventy.

Where did everybody go?

When you look at your own, and hear their laughter, and feel the weight and truth of them upon the inverted horse you have become for them, you know as well as any man has every known that you have everything.

You have your old self, you have your sons and daughters: you have their sons and daughters, you have your history, your memories, your daily schedule, and your plans, all in a world of peace.

War?
What war?
Bomb?
What bomb?
Madness?
What madness?
If these things are everywhere, they are not here.
If these things must destroy everything, I know nothing about it.
I have only lived.
I still live.
Something very slow and lasting happens when lightning strikes dust into a human

being.